A TIME OF GRACE – SCHOOL MEMORIES

Edmund Rice
and
the Presentation Tradition of Education

Edited by J. Matthew Feheney FPM

VERITAS

First published 1996 by
Veritas Publications
7-8 Lower Abbey Street
Dublin 1

Compilation copyright © J. Matthew Feheney 1996

ISBN I 85390 356 6

British Library Cataloguing
in Publication Data.
A catalogue record for
this book is available
from the British Library.

Cover design by Bill Bolger
Printed in the Republic of Ireland by Betaprint Ltd, Dublin

CONTENTS

FOREWORD

J. Matthew Feheney FPM

This book is one of several published to mark the beatification of Edmund Rice on 5 October 1996. It seeks to explore and examine the spirit and tradition of Edmund Rice within the Congregation of the Presentation Brothers, one of two Congregations which he founded, the other being that of the Christian Brothers.

We realise that Edmund Rice's name is generally associated with the more widely known Christian Brothers. The fact remains, however, that the original Congregation founded by Edmund was known for the first twenty years as the Society of the Presentation and its members were known variously as Presentation Brothers, Presentation Monks or Gentlemen of the Presentation.

Two traditions
The personality, charism and genius of Edmund Rice comes, therefore, to us from two traditions: the tradition of the Christian Brothers and the tradition of the Presentation Brothers. Of the two, much more has been written about the Christian Brothers. The Presentation story, on the other hand, has been somewhat neglected. Publications since the early years of this century, including articles, newsletters and journals, have been both occasional and in-house, designed to cater for the needs of the Brothers themselves. Allen's first volume – *The Presentation Brothers* – of a planned two-volume study, did not appear until 1993 and, though a fine piece of scholarship, was also intended for private circulation only. Apart from vocations promotion material, therefore, there has hitherto been no significant attempt to bring the story of Edmund Rice and the Presentation Brothers before the public at large.

It goes without saying that the responsibility for this omission lies primarily, if not exclusively, with the Presentation Brothers themselves. In the past, religious Congregations like the Presentation Brothers did not feel the need to explain themselves and their mission to the public. However, the widespread interest in Edmund Rice which was stimulated by the news that he was to be beatified in October 1996 served to make the Presentation Brothers aware of the fact that they have a significant public, including parents, teachers, past students and friends, who are eager to learn more about them and their connection with Edmund Rice.

As has been pointed out in another article in this volume, 'Edmund Rice and the Presentation Brothers', the original religious society founded by Edmund evolved into two separate Congregations. The impetus for this evolution was Edmund's decision to reorganise the original society along the lines of the French Brothers of the Christian Schools, founded by John Baptist De La Salle. While, over a period of time, the vast majority of Edmund's confrères accepted the new development, a small minority in Cork chose to adhere to the old Presentation Rule and to remain under the direct authority of the Bishop, continuing to be known as the Presentation Brothers.

While this small group, of which we know the name of only one member, would maintain that they continued the original Society, some historians from the Christian Brothers tradition have viewed them as a new Congregation. This interpretation of the relevant events would not be acceptable to the Presentation Brothers. The latter would contend, as does the present writer, that the adoption of the Rule, customs and name of the French Brothers of the Christian Schools introduced a new element to Edmund's original society. To some degree at least, it diluted the original Irish tradition of the Congregation through the adoption of an ethos and spirit that was French, being that of the French Brothers of the Christian Schools. As a corollary, I would also suggest that the ethos and spirit of the minority, which persisted with the original Presentation way of life, preserved important aspects of the original inspiration of Edmund Rice, as well as arguably being more in keeping with Irish spirituality. The reader is invited to evaluate and judge for him/herself the ethos and spirit that comes through from the simple and candid accounts of the contributors to this volume.

All the contributors are laymen connected with the Presentation Brothers either as past students, teachers or associates. We regret that there are no women among the contributors. It is probable that, with greater foresight, this omission could have been avoided, though the fact remains that it is only relatively recently that women teachers have been employed to any significant extent in schools of the Presentation Brothers and, moreover, that few of these schools are as yet co-educational. The position has, however, drastically changed during the past five years with the introduction of the Presentation Associate programme. There seems no doubt, therefore, that women will play a much more significant part in the future of the Presentation Brothers and the Presentation extended family. Frank Steele's article in this volume, 'Presentation 2000', sketches the background against which we hope this involvement will become possible.

Presentation tradition
In the original letter inviting contributions, writers were asked to reflect on the ethos and spirit which they detected and perceived during their school days and attempt to articulate it. Different contributors have approached this task in different ways. Some have concentrated on describing and analysing their own school experiences, occasionally taking a look at the underlying system. Others have given pen pictures of individual teachers and of typical events. Yet others have provided an overview in chronicle form. The poems included are a special feature and I will say a separate word about them below.

Arrangement of articles
Apart from the poems and a few pieces giving general information about the Presentation Brothers (Feheney, Lucky and Steele), the articles are arranged in chronological order of the periods discussed, starting with the nineteenth century and ending with the 1980s. This makes it possible to evaluate the ethos and spirit in each generation. It is immediately obvious that there was a very close relationship between some of the Brothers and their students during the nineteenth century. Brother Paul

Townsend (1798-1880) had a remarkable effect on his students. He emerges from the descriptions of his past students as a much loved and esteemed gentleman. Here was a man of culture and accomplishment whose dedication to the education of poor children was, nevertheless, never in question.

Nineteenth century

Joseph Conroy's contribution on 'Greenmount in the 1870s' is an extraordinary piece, not only as a historical document but also as a detailed account of the way an Irish orphanage was run during that period. The similarities between this orphanage and the best public schools in England come to mind. Brother Baptist of Greenmount emerges as an innovator reminiscent of the great Thomas Arnold of Rugby School. But Brother Baptist had a rapport with his boys that was foreign to the aloof and unbending Arnold. Moreover, even Arnold made use of the rod on occasion. This piece is full of points of special interest, which merits closer study, for which, regretfully, we do not have time or space in this volume.

Sean O'Faolain

Sean O'Faolain's piece from his autobiography, *Vive Moi*, is included because it is helpful as a critical background against which to place some of the articles by later students of Presentation College, Cork, popularly known as Pres. O'Faolain is critical of Pres. Writing more than forty years later, he judges the Pres of his time against the best educational institutions he has encountered in literature as well as in life. He calls Pres a fake because, in his opinion, it was both snobbish and a cram school. Though few would argue that O'Faolain's criticism in this instance, any more than in others, should be taken at full face value, it is, nevertheless, helpful in assessing the contribution of his old school to education in Cork and in the country as a whole. It certainly makes a positive contribution towards the purpose of the present volume, which is to articulate and reflect on the Christian ethos of the school and evaluate to what extent it exemplified the charism and spirit of Edmund Rice and his early followers. Such an approach inevitably entails facing and accepting the negatives as well as celebrating the positives.

O'Faolain acknowledges the lifelong influence of Pres on him. He singles out three teachers, who, for him, symbolised the good and bad aspects of the school. Moreover, he paints an attractive picture of each of these three men, the dominating figure being Brother E.J. Connolly, known throughout Cork as The Man.

1930s & 1940s

Writing about the Pres of his time, Dan Donovan also recalls Brother Connolly: Dan had a unique association with the school, covering almost sixty years starting when he was a small boy and ending when he was Vice-Principal.

Cecil Hurwitz recalls his conversion from Judaism while in Pres and reminds us that many Jewish boys attended the school and were always made to feel welcome. Edmund Van Esbeck, the well-known sports journalist and author, reviews the contribution of Pres to rugby in Cork and Ireland. Sean Maher's contribution describes a different world: that of the Industrial School, about which many former students seem to have unpleasant memories. For Sean, however, his stay in Greenmount was a little bit of heaven. It enabled him to escape from the hardship and misery of wandering the roads of Ireland as a traveller. Sean had an extraordinary thirst for knowledge and in Brother Eugene Sheehan he found the guru of his dreams. Brother Eugene was sympathetic to his culture and eager to introduce him to the world of literature and the pleasures of reading. Sean's book, *The Road to God Knows Where*, is a classic of its kind and deserves reprinting.

Liam Mac Mathúna, writing in Irish, recalls his time in the Presentation Brothers Juniorate in Cork. It was during this period that he acquired his lifelong dedication to Irish. This, however, was not imposed from the top down but was evidently an expression of the spirit and aspirations of the young people themselves.

1950s & 1960s

John McGahern regards his school days at Presentation College, Carrick-on-Shannon, as 'a time of grace – actual grace'. In the course of his article, he recalls the late Brother Damien Hanley reminding the boys in the College that they should always make it clear that they were students of the Presentation Brothers, not of the more widely known Christian Brothers.

> Brother Damien was very keen that we – or anybody else – should never confuse the Presentation with the Christian Brothers. 'My dear boys', he used to tell us as we prepared to scatter for the summer holidays, 'you will meet people who will assume, once they hear you are attending the Brothers, that *we* are the Christian Brothers. Now, enlighten these people on my behalf that you are *not* attending the Christian Brothers, and that you may be Christian in the sense that you are not pagan, but in no other sense.'

John himself has always been at pains to make this point. It would appear that both he and his old teacher, Brother Damian, felt that this clarification was in some way important in the expression of their own identity. It is also an important point for most Presentation Brothers, who, while freely acknowledging that the Christian Brothers surpass them in numbers and accomplishments, nevertheless rejoice in their own separate ethos and identity.

We get a glimpse of the extraordinary bonds established between teacher and pupils in Liam Nolan's contribution. Though the personalities of Kevin and Eugenius were miles apart, each weaved his own magic spell: Kevin by empathy and affirmation, Eugenius by introducing his pupils to the world of the imagination as he gazed out at the natural beauty of the magnificent harbour in Cobh, while declaiming his favourite Robert Service ballads. Alan Titley, in the course of his recollections, makes an evaluation of the education he received at Coláiste Chríost Rí, Cork. Writing from his present perspective as a senior lecturer in education at one of our premier colleges of education, Alan has neither regrets nor 'chips' about his school days. He has some very cogent and commonsense remarks to make about school ethos and mission statements. Michael J. Kelleher and John Fraher recall their school days from the perspective of their present standing as leaders in research at university level. Both are candid in their observations and assessment of the Pres of their time. Michael Kelleher looks into the future and envisages a time when there will be no Presentation Brother in that hallowed establishment and rightly points out the need to put structures in place to ensure the continuance of the good and desirable features.

Jim Cremin's contribution about school memories during this period is focused on his first day in school and on the endearing, if unorthodox, Brother Ailbie O'Connor. In his own way, Ailbie was also an innovator. Not for him the points race and the winning of scholarships but a warm welcome for each child in his junior infant class, starting with a good fire, a mug of cocoa and a giant bun encrusted with delicious icing. Ailbie had his own unique way of building self-confidence and empowering his young charges.

Pat Coffey has had the opportunity to look at the Presentation tradition from several perspectives. He experienced it in primary school, in secondary school, as a young Presentation Brother who worked in England and Canada as well as in Ireland, as a teacher for twenty-two years in a Presentation school, as the father of two boys attending a Presentation school and, more recently, as a Department of Education Inspector. Pat believes there is a special Presentation ethos and that the charism of Edmund Rice continues to be mediated in a special way through the Presentation tradition.

1970s & 1980s

Declan Kennedy has been in contact with the Presentation Brothers in Cobh since he was a small boy, initially as a student and subsequently as a teacher. He obviously made many friends among the Brothers and is virtually, if not actually, a member of the extended Presentation family. Both Kieran Groeger and Fergal Keane write about their recollections of Presentation College, Cork. Despite the great rugby tradition of the school, neither sought self-fulfilment in this area. Kieran, however, recalls some of the rugby songs and captures some of the excitement surrounding the great rugby matches of his day.

Fergal Keane recalls SHARE, that inspiring schoolboy charity founded by Brother Jerome Kelly while he was Principal of Pres. Fergal paints a picture of a school helping a young man to find himself and to discern his own gifts. SHARE evidently helped provide a channel for his own deep social commitment, something which he was subsequently able to express to a world-wide audience during his coverage of South Africa, Rwanda and the Far East as a BBC correspondent.

Poets and poems

In these pages, interspersed between articles, is included the work of three notable Cork poets, two of whom are past students of the Presentation Brothers, the third being a teacher at Presentation College, Cork. The senior by age is Patrick Galvin, born in the late 1920s, and a former pupil of the historic South Monastery, Cork. Patrick, now something of a father figure for younger poets in Cork, also has memories of a period when talents such as his received little recognition and less financial support. Thank God for the bursaries, fellowships and awards which have since then become available to young poets.

William Wall, in the longer of his two poems, recalls the death of one of his students, tragically knocked down and killed during a school holiday in France.

Greg Delanty, though a Cork man born and bred, teaches at St Michael's College, Winooski, Canada. The poems reprinted in this volume are, however, redolent of Cork.

This book is intended for the general reader rather than for academics. In keeping with this objective I have tried to keep references and notes to a minimum. I thank all our contributors for responding to our initial invitation to contribute and, subsequently, for meeting deadlines. Thanks also to Fiona Biggs of Veritas, for overseeing publication. Finally, thanks to the members of the extended Presentation Family, for whom this book is primarily intended, for their commitment to the mission of Edmund Rice and their fidelity to the Presentation tradition.

EDMUND RICE AND THE PRESENTATION BROTHERS[1]

J. Matthew Feheney FPM

Edmund Rice, founder of both the Presentation and Christian Brothers, was born in Callan, Co. Kilkenny, on 1 June 1762. He came from a large family of seven boys. He also had two step-sisters, children of his mother by a previous marriage. His father was a farmer with almost two hundred acres of land, leased from a local Protestant landlord, Lord Desart. In comparison with the majority of Irish Catholics of the period, his family were considered 'well-off'.

Early education
In common with the practice of the time, Edmund was taught his prayers and the basics of his religion by his mother at home. At the age of seven he began to attend a local hedge school in Callan. The name hedge was derisory since these schools were usually accommodated in little thatched houses, called cabins, which were often used as mass houses on Sundays.

School in Kilkenny
The deplorable physical amenities of the hedge school did not, however, prevent Edmund from quickly mastering the 'three Rs', and, at the age of fifteen, he moved on to a more advanced school in Kilkenny, operated by a Mr White, a Catholic. Here the curriculum included 'Mathematics, Latin, Greek, French, Grammar, Book-keeping, Globes, Maps, Drawing, Music and Fencing'. We do not know whether Edmund took all these subjects, but, being a conscientious young man, he probably took most of them. There is a tradition that he excelled at mathematics and book-keeping. Moreover, the progress he was making in his studies, allied to his natural courtesy and good manners, attracted the attention of his uncle, Michael Rice, a successful merchant and ship's chandler in Waterford.

Into business

Edmund's uncle, Michael, was so impressed with his nephew that he invited him to join him as an apprentice in his business. With the full approval of his parents, Edmund accepted this generous invitation and, before long, he was his uncle's right-hand assistant. Though Michael Rice had two sons of his own, neither was interested in their father's business. His nephew, Edmund, on the other hand, had a great flair for it: he was quick at figures, he was a good organiser and he got on well with people. After a few years it became obvious to Uncle Michael that his nephew was the most suitable person to succeed him in charge of the business and, when he died, it was no surprise to anyone that Edmund inherited it.

A bright future

A bright future stretched ahead of Edmund: though not yet thirty years of age, he already owned a flourishing business. His knowledge of business and legal affairs and his prudence and sound judgement were beginning to be recognised and appreciated by his growing circle of friends. In 1787 his own father, Robert Rice, chose Edmund to draw up his will, making him executor of it, even though Edmund was then only twenty-five years of age and the fourth son in the family. This was just one of the many instances where people showed their confidence in his skill and integrity. As the years went by, he would be called on by many people to execute their wills, to invest their money and to make legal representations on their behalf.

Marriage and tragedy

At the age of twenty-three, Edmund married a young woman, thought to be named Mary Elliott, the daughter of a well-to-do neighbour. Little is known for certain about her, though tradition says that she was outgoing and vivacious with a great love of horse-riding. About a year after the marriage she died suddenly. Some say her death was the result of a fall from a horse while out riding, others from a fever. She was pregnant at the time and, before she died, she gave birth to a baby girl, also named Mary, who seems to have been handicapped.

Edmund's world seemed to collapse about him: in one cruel blow fate deprived him of his much-loved wife and gave him instead a handicapped daughter.

Prayer and the Bible
Though initially overcome by grief, Edmund soon accepted with resignation the cross laid on him by a Providence he firmly believed to be compassionate and loving. It brought home to him the transient nature of human joy and the need to look beyond this life for lasting happiness. Though his business flourished under his wise and painstaking management, he began to give more attention to his spiritual life. He acquired his own copy of the Bible and began to read it daily. He underlined texts which made a deep impression on him and returned to these again and again. Always a practical man, he paid special attention to what the Bible had to say about honesty in business affairs, especially Exodus 22:25; Proverbs 22:16; Ezekiel 13:21; Matthew 5:42 and Luke 6:35.

Charitable works
Edmund took an active part in the charitable work of his adopted city of Waterford. When two young Connolly girls suddenly became orphans, Edmund had them reared and educated at his own expense. When the Gaelic poet, Tadhg Gaelach O'Sullivan, underwent a religious conversion and wished to publish a book of religious poems in a *Pious Miscellany*, Edmund was one of those who subscribed to the publication of the volume. He was also a signatory to a petition to King George III protesting against the wording of the Oath of Allegiance which Catholics found offensive. This petition was forwarded to His Majesty by a committee of the people of Waterford in 1792 and was one of the events that helped to prepare the climate for the Relief Act of 1793. But one of his most enduring and enlightened actions was to negotiate a lease for the site of Presentation Convent, Waterford, on 1 June 1799. This was Edmund's first encounter with the spiritual daughters of Nano Nagle, a woman he greatly admired and whose example he was eventually to emulate.

Soon after they were established in Waterford, the Presentation

Sisters had to call on Edmund Rice again for advice about their financial affairs. Edmund invested their small capital so as to give the best possible dividend. In return, the Sisters loaned him a copy of their Rule, and he studied it with more than casual curiosity.

Works of mercy

Meantime, Edmund had begun to attend daily Mass and to read religious books. In the year 1794 he and some friends founded a society for visiting the sick and lonely as well as helping them out financially. As this work expanded it brought him into contact with the poor people living in the slums of Waterford. He was especially touched at the sight of many young boys who were not attending school and were growing up, not only ignorant of their religion, but also unable to read or write and without discipline or restraint of any kind. Today, we might call them juvenile delinquents. The only free schools were Protestant and the teachers in those felt they were entitled to proselytise any Catholic pupils who attended. True, there were some small private Catholic schools but they charged fees and were intended for the children of more prosperous Catholics. Free primary education, as we know it today, was as yet unheard of in Ireland.

Ministry to poor boys

Very soon Edmund, though engaged in business during the day, began a ministry of his own in the evenings. When he finished work he would open up his own house to poor boys, giving them meals and teaching them their prayers and catechism. He also gave lessons in reading and writing to those boys who were interested. When he saw their tattered clothes, Edmund's business training and flair came to the rescue: he purchased a bale of cloth, hired a tailor and had him make suits for the boys. Shoes were his next venture: he purchased the leather in bulk and hired a shoemaker to make shoes for his charges.

Starting in a stable

As the number of boys increased, Edmund looked around for larger premises. He purchased a building, formerly used as a stable, with good stone walls, and made the ground floor into a class-room, while upstairs he made space for the tailor and shoemaker. This was Edmund Rice's first school. It provided what the pupils wanted: clothing, shoes and education. But soon he became aware of the fact the boys were sometimes hungry. So his next venture was a bakery. Now, in addition to the other things, the boys could be sure of a good meal.

The search for good teachers

Though Edmund was the first teacher of these boys, as the tailor's shop, the shoemaker's shop and the bakery developed, he had less time for teaching so he looked around for helpers. It was comparatively easy to find a tailor, a shoemaker and a baker, but finding teachers proved more difficult, not least because the boys were very rough and difficult to control. The teachers whom he initially engaged gave up in frustration and departed and, for a while, the future of the project seemed in danger. But Edmund put his trust in Providence and, when things seemed hopeless, two young men arrived from his native Callan offering their services and asking to join him in his work. These first companions attracted others and Edmund's school prospered and grew.

Religious congregation

Meantime, however, he began to feel the call to give up his business and devote himself full-time to the work of educating poor boys. The ecclesiastical rules of the day demanded that any religious group requiring approval from Rome had to live a monastic life and wear religious habit. Inspired by the example of Nano Nagle, Edmund attended the first Mass celebrated in the new Presentation Convent Waterford on the Feast of St Joseph, 19 March 1801. One year later, in 1802, he took the historic decision to found a small community of Brothers of the Presentation. He had studied the Presentation Rule of the religious sisters of Nano Nagle and had come to the conclusion that God was calling him and his companions to do for poor boys what these charitable women had done for poor girls.

Much suffering

Edmund's decision to found a religious congregation ensured that there would be a steady stream of young men joining him to continue his work. Initially the group was called the Society of the Presentation, the members being popularly known as the Monks of the Presentation and, also, as the Gentlemen of the Presentation. In 1803 Edmund built a new monastery and school in Ballybricken, outside the walls of the city of Waterford, and named it Mount Sion. Here, he and his companions made vows of chastity, poverty and obedience in 1808, and began to wear a black habit – indoors only, because the Penal Laws, though somewhat relaxed, were still on the statute books, and they forbade the wearing of any religious garb by Roman Catholics.

Spreading out from Waterford

As the number of volunteers joining Edmund increased, he acceded to requests from priests and bishops in other towns and dioceses to open schools. Soon there was a network of them: Carrick-on-Suir (1806), Dungarvan (1807), Cork (1811), Dublin (1812), Limerick (1816), Thurles (1816) Preston (1825).

Many sufferings

Edmund encountered many difficulties in the second half of his life. Certain members of the clergy and some bishops opposed him, while some Brothers in his own Congregation suspected, misunderstood and even made false allegations against him. Eventually, he offered his resignation as leader and this was promptly accepted. But he cheerfully accepted each of these crosses, just as he had the death of his beloved wife and the handicap of his daughter, Mary. He believed that God purifies with suffering those whom he has specially chosen.

Death

Edmund died at Mount Sion, Waterford, on 29 August 1844. In April 1993 Pope John Paul II declared him venerable. This, however, was merely a preliminary step to his beatification on 6 October 1996. The decision to beatify Edmund came at the end of a long investigation into his life and work and after the acceptance of a certified miracle attributed to his intercession. Edmund, like many other saintly people, was purified in the crucible of suffering and it is not only his great success as the founder of a world-wide network of schools for poor children that inspires people, but also his patient and cheerful acceptance of the many sufferings God sent him. Nor must it be thought that what he achieved was accomplished because the circumstances were ideal or the odds always in his favour: no, indeed! It was, rather, because of his perseverance and heroic efforts. Indeed, it could be said that many of his good deeds and achievements were effected *in spite* of difficulties, misunderstandings and opposition.

Revered in Waterford
A Waterford Quaker who witnessed Edmund's funeral summed up his life with remarkable insight:

> The display of feelings manifested at the interment of Brother Rice shows that the people are neither forgetful nor ungrateful. No wonder, as they see the extraordinary change brought about mainly by his instrumentality. The Roman Catholics believe he was a messenger from God.... Mr Rice is not dead! He lives! Yes, he lives the highest, noblest and greatest life. He lives in the noble band of Christian workmen to whom he has bequeathed his spirit and his work. (Normoyle, 414)

Brothers of the Presentation to Cork
Soon after Edmund Rice founded his Society of the Presentation in Waterford, Bishop Moylan of Cork got to hear of it and determined to establish a branch in Cork. In 1804 he sent a postulant named Sheridan to Waterford but this young man did not persevere in his vocation. In 1809 Bishop Moylan paid a personal visit to Mount Sion and was so impressed with the class discipline and teaching methods of the Brothers and the conduct of the children that, on his return to Cork, he called a special meeting of the committee of the Cork Charitable Society, which managed no fewer than nine schools for poor children in Cork at the time.

At this meeting Bishop Moylan outlined the miseries of the

poor in Cork and the need to provide their children with a good basic schooling. He was convinced that only people who were strongly committed to their faith and had both the requisite knowledge and classroom skills could accomplish this work satisfactorily. The committee had experienced many difficulties in finding suitable teachers for its schools in recent years and had encountered some who proved unsatisfactory. Following Bishop Moylan's appeal, the following resolution was adopted at a subsequent meeting of the committee on 25 February 1810:

> It was also resolved that the sum of one hundred pounds shall be applied to the purpose of sending two young men who shall be approved of by the Bishop and the clergymen of this committee to the monastery in Waterford in order to have them fitted for an Establishment of a similar nature in this city. (Allen, 35)

Two young men, Jeremiah O'Connor and John Leonard, volunteered their services and were accepted and, on St Patrick's Day 1810, proceeded to Mount Sion, Waterford, where they received their religious and teacher training under the personal supervision of Edmund Rice. In November 1811 they returned to Cork, having been professed as Brothers of the Presentation before leaving Waterford.

Success of the first school in Cork

On their return to Cork the two young men were given charge of the Cork Charitable Society's North School, then situated off Chapel Lane, in the shadow of the North Chapel (now Cathedral). They found accommodation in nearby Clarence Street. The school was small and badly in need of repair and their own accommodation less than adequate.

When the Brothers took over management of the school in Chapel Lane there were two teachers and seventeen pupils, who were reported to be very undisciplined. Shortly afterwards they were joined by Brother Francis Ryan, also trained in Waterford, and, the following March, by Patrick Leonard, brother of John, who had considerable experience of working in a bank. By mid –

1814 Michael McDermott and Michael Augustine Riordan had joined them. There were now six Brothers on the staff teaching arithmetic, reading and spelling, geometry and mensuration and book-keeping. From seventeen boys in 1811 the numbers had jumped to 450 in 1815. Meantime the Brothers had moved into more congenial quarters in Peacock Lane. Later, they went to live in the new North Monastery, designed and built by one of their Brothers, Michael Augustine Riordan. In 1818 they moved into the new North Monastery school also built by Brother Riordan.

Hunger, typhus and debt
Unfortunately, this period of expansion coincided with a general failure of the potato crop, the staple diet of the people. The hunger and starvation of 1816-17, coupled with overcrowding in the tenements of the poor, led to a severe outbreak of typhus throughout the city and thousands died. The fever hospitals were completely inadequate to meet the situation. In this emergency, the Brothers handed over their new school to the city authorities to be used as a temporary fever hospital. The Brothers themselves suffered severely, subsisting on potatoes and milk, not being able to afford meat. Were it not for the charity of the Lyons family, they would have been hungry. As it was, Brother Francis Ryan died of typhus and Brother Ignatius McDermott of the 'decline', as tuberculosis was then known.

Though helped by the Cork Charitable Society, the Brothers went into debt to erect the new buildings on the new site of the North Monastery. It was a particularly bad time to incur a debt in Cork. In addition to an extended recession following the end of the Napoleonic wars, which affected the country as a whole, there were the mini-famine and typhus outbreak in Cork. The latter affected the earning power of the community by directly causing the death of one of the Brothers while it is very likely that under-nourishment contributed to the death of the other. This debt was to be a burden on the Cork community for many years to come.

Bishop Murphy

Bishop Moylan died in 1815 and his successor as Bishop of Cork was Dr John Murphy, whose family was in the brewing industry and whose brother founded the Ladywell brewery which made Murphy's Stout. He was a very interesting man, a bibliophile, a patron of Gaelic poets and scholars, as well as a man of independent means. He owned the largest library in Cork. He was also, however, a man of strong opinions and convictions.

The De La Salle French Rule

One of the problems the Brothers encountered under the Presentation Rule was that there was no provision for the transfer of Brothers from a house in one diocese to a house in another diocese. To cater for this possibility, a chapter in Waterford in 1809 introduced an article into the Rule which made provision for it. Nevertheless, even with this provision, misunderstandings arose between Bishops, creating difficulties for the Brothers. With this in mind, Dr Murray, Coadjutor Archbishop of Dublin, visited the mother house of the De La Salle or Brothers of the Christian Schools in Paris and obtained from the Superior General a copy of their Rules and Constitutions and Bull of approval. Encouraged by Dr Murray, Edmund Rice studied these documents and found that transfer from one diocese to another was not a problem for the De La Salle Brothers. This was because it was a pontifical institute directly responsible to the Pope and governed by a Superior General and Council elected by the Brothers themselves. As a pontifical institute, it was independent of the local bishop in the administration of its own affairs and answerable directly to Rome.

The De La Salle Rules and Constitutions were translated into English and a copy sent to each house, to be studied and discussed by the Brothers. After allowing sufficient time to study the documents a meeting of superiors was arranged in Mount Sion, Waterford, in August, 1817. All the superiors, with the exception of the house in Cork, attended and even the Cork house sent a representative in place of the superior. There was general agreement with the spirit of the De La Salle rules and Constitutions but adaptations were suggested and accepted to suit local circumstances. It was agreed, however, that no further action would be taken until the local bishops were consulted.

In June 1818 the Rules and Constitutions adopted at the Waterford meeting the previous year were forwarded to Rome together with a testimonial from Archbishop Troy of Dublin. Three years later Rome replied with a Brief from Pope Pius VII. All the professed Brothers were summoned to Thurles on 25 August 1821 to hear this read. There were nineteen professed members present and three unable to attend. Though a few voiced the opinion that the Brief gave too much authority to the Superior General, the majority accepted it and a vote to this effect was carried with a large majority.

Cork Brothers resist amalgamation

The Cork Brothers were not present at the Thurles meeting, presumably in deference to the wishes of their Bishop, who opposed the Brief. Dr Walsh, the new bishop of Waterford also opposed it, but the Archbishops of Dublin and Cashel were in favour. A further meeting was called in Waterford on 20 January 1822, to formally accept the Brief. Most of the professed Brothers and novices attended and pronounced their vows in accordance with the Brief. Nine professed Brothers and two novices, however, were absent. Six of those who were absent later accepted the Brief while three left the Society. Of the remaining two, one, Ignatius Mulcahy of Cappoquin, continued to live out his life in that town as a Brother of the Society of the Presentation. The other, Michael Augustine Riordan, as we shall see below, was instrumental in continuing the original Society of the Presentation in accordance with the Presentation Rule under the direct authority of Bishop Murphy of Cork.

The Cork House, now located in the North Monastery, remained disconnected from Edmund for some years. In 1823 the Superior, Brother Jerome O'Connor, left for Waterford where he formally accepted the Brief and was professed accordingly. The senior members, however, including Brothers John and Patrick Leonard and Michael Augustine Riordan, as yet made no move in that direction.

Brother Michael Augustine Riordan, as the Bishop's chief

adviser in architectural affairs, was devoted to the Bishop. The Leonards, however, were wary of him. Their wariness seemed to be justified when, in 1826, Bishop Murphy demanded a Deed of Assignment relating to the community property in Peacock Lane, Cork, something which would give him ownership of it. The Leonards refused to accede to this request unless both their names were also included in the deed. The Bishop would not agree to this. While hitherto the Leonards hesitated to accept the Brief in deference to the wishes of Bishop Murphy, what to them seemed his unreasonable demand for ownership of the community property in Peacock Lane tilted the scales in favour of accepting the Brief. In the minds of the Leonards, Bishop Murphy could not be relied upon to protect the interests of the new Congregation.

In May 1826 John B. Leonard paid a visit to Waterford where he accepted the Brief and made his vows accordingly. His brother, Patrick J., did likewise in June while Paul Riordan, not to be confused with Michael Augustine Riordan, the architect, followed suit later the same month. Now only Michael Augustine Riordan remained under the direct authority of the Bishop of Cork.

Cork community splits

In the autumn of 1826 Bishop Murphy paid a visit to the North Monastery and inquired if the Brothers had any complaint against his treatment of them. They all replied that they had not and that only the interests of the institute induced them to accept the Brief. The Annals of the South Monastery, Cork, describe the scene:

> Then the Bishop turned to Michael A. Riordan and another who were very dear friends of his, he appealed to them to remain under his jurisdiction, and said that he would make special arrangements to suit the case. His appeal succeeded. The two severed their connection with the Brothers of the North Monastery to the very great regret of the Community. (Allen, 51)

It should be noted that it was loyalty to Bishop Murphy, not any animosity towards Edmund Rice or his confrères, which impelled Brother Michael Augustine Riordan and his companion to part company with the North Monastery community. Though the juridical link between the two groups was finally severed in 1826, the all-important spiritual connection, the Presentation Rule, which nurtured Edmund and his religious family for the first twenty years, was retained. This was the Rule, which, with minor changes, was observed by the Presentation Brothers until after Vatican II.

Presentation Brothers at South Monastery
After leaving the North Monastery in the autumn of 1826, Brother Michael Augustine Riordan and at least one unnamed companion, moved to the South Parish, Cork. On 1 July 1827 he and some companions opened a school in Cat Lane off Barrack Street, Cork and before long they had an enrolment of four hundred pupils. The Bishop gave them part of the recently vacated South Presentation Convent as their home, the remaining part being used temporarily as a presbytery for the parish clergy until they moved to nearby Dunbar Street. When this happened the Brothers took out a long lease of the entire former Presentation Convent and grounds in Douglas Street, which they renamed the South Monastery, Cork.

Brother Michael Augustine Riordan, the architect, then began building a new school in the grounds of the South Monastery. He received two important financial contributions that helped him establish a suitable base for his new community and school. One was £500 from Dean Collins, Parish Priest of the South Parish, and the other a similar sum from the Ursuline Sisters in Blackrock, Cork. This latter amount was part contribution and part payment for Brother Riordan's services as architect in the erection of a large extension to the Ursuline convent in Blackrock. When the new school at the South Monastery was completed the pupils in the Cat Lane school were transferred there.

Presentation Brothers expand

In October 1827 Brother Riordan was entrusted with the direction of the Lancasterian School in Washington Street, Cork. This school, in operation since 1814, was under the management of the Cork Charitable Society and was already in association with the National Board of Education. It consisted of one very large classroom, ninety feet long and sixty feet wide, and was very much in demand for large meetings and banquets. One of the largest held there was a Repeal meeting in April 1844 for Daniel O'Connell and six hundred guests.

In 1838 Brother Michael Augustine Riordan, with the approval of the Bishop of Cork, acceded to a request from Bishop Egan of Kerry to establish a Presentation Brothers monastery in Killarney. This was followed by a similar foundation in nearby Milltown in 1842. In the mid-1840s groups of Brothers were also sent, again with the approval of the Bishop of Cork, to establish missions to Madras in India, and Pittsburgh in Pennsylvania, both of which, despite initial success, soon came to an end because of lack of personnel. Brother Riordan died in 1848 and was succeeded as Superior by Brother Paul Townsend, whose life and career are discussed elsewhere in this volume.

Architectural contribution to Diocese of Cork

Brother Michael Augustine Riordan's death notice states that he was the architect of many of the churches in the dioceses of Cork and Cloyne. Though endowed with great talent, he was a man of great humility and his name was not publicly associated with many of his buildings. In addition to the school in the South Monastery, the house and school in the North Monastery and the Ursuline Convent in Blackrock, a list of the buildings for which he was architect included the following: St Michael's, Blackrock; St John the Baptist, Ovens; St Patrick's, Doneraile; St Patrick's, Dunmanway; St Finbarr's, Bantry; parish church, Millstreet; St John the Baptist, Kinsale; St Patrick's, Skibbereen; St Mary's, Rossmore; St Fachtna's, Rosscarbery; St Mary's, Leap; St Joseph's, Castletown-Kenneith.

Presentation houses amalgamate

In 1856 Brother Paul Townsend opened a school in Gallows Green, Cork, which he renamed Greenmount in an attempt to end the association of the place with public executions. In 1868 the Presentation Brothers took over the administration of St Patrick's Orphanage, Greenmount, established by a committee under the Bishop a few years previously. In 1874 they built St Joseph's Industrial School, Greenmount, which remained in operation until 1959. Brother Townsend died in 1880, bringing to an end the direct connection with Bishop Murphy, who had played such a crucial role in the division of the Cork Community and the continuation of Society of the Presentation as Edmund Rice had first envisaged it.

Brother Paul Townsend had, however, trained up a new group of Presentation Brothers who saw the wisdom of amalgamating all the Presentation houses and schools under their own Superior General. In 1889 they held a chapter and took the momentous decision to seek approval from the Pope to amalgamate and become a pontifical institute united under a Superior General of their own choosing. They were supported in this decision by Bishop O'Callaghan of Cork and Bishop Coffin of Southwark. Brother Patrick Shine was elected first Superior General and served from 1889 until his death in 1905.

Presentation Rule and name retained

Though the Presentation Brothers waited until 1889 to amalgamate and adopt a form of self-government juridically analogous to that chosen by Edmund Rice and the majority of his companions in 1822, there was one important difference. This was the Presentation Rule. In 1822 Edmund and majority of his companions had chosen to adopt the French De La Salle Rule, after which they became popularly known as the Brothers of the Christian Schools of Ireland generally shortened to the Irish Christian Brothers. The small group, led by Brother Michael Augustine Riordan, which left the North Monastery, Cork, in the autumn of 1826, on the other hand, retained both the Presentation Rule and Presentation name and their successors continued to adhere to both after they had become a pontifical institute in 1889.

Different traditions

It is obvious that while the Presentation and Christian Brothers are both spiritual sons of Edmund Rice, there are some differences between them. While the Congregation of the Christian Brothers had an unbroken association with Edmund Rice, the adoption of the De La Salle Rule and many De La Salle customs introduced, especially after Edmund's death in 1844, a French spirit that was not always in harmony with the Irish genius. The effects of this French influence manifested themselves in various ways in the educational philosophy and teaching style of the Christian Brothers over almost two centuries but have yet to be identified and evaluated by historians. Moreover, the personality, charism and heritage of Edmund himself has also been mediated by the Christian Brothers through an Irish-French ethos and spirituality, thereby running the risk of losing some of the force, vigour and attractiveness of the man himself.

The Presentation Brothers on the other hand lost direct contact with Edmund in 1826. The picture of Edmund they retained was that of the vigorous, middle-aged, retired businessman turned founder, before his later eclipse and rejection by what might be termed the pro-De La Salle faction in his council. Brother Michael Augustine Riordan had many of the qualities and a good deal of the style of Edmund Rice: he was a leader and an organiser with many talents: architect, builder, supervisor, teacher, school superintendent. He encouraged initiative among his confrères and depended a good deal on them to accomplish his mission. He was modest and forgetful of self while loath to publicise his accomplishments and achievements. During his later years his vigour and effectiveness were greatly reduced by ill-health.

Presentation spirituality was unadulteratedly Irish and was rooted in Edmund's original Society of the Presentation, influenced as this was by Nano Nagle and the Presentation Sisters. The Presentation educational ethos was pragmatic, adaptable, ready to co-operate with other agencies and pupil-centred, while, arguably, lacking the French flair for organisation. It is well exemplified in the approach and educational career of Brother Paul Townsend.

Providence
There is no doubt that it was in the providence of God that the original group founded by Edmund Rice should evolve into two related but separate Congregations, the Presentation and Christian Brothers. Each has preserved in its own unique way the charism and inspiration of Edmund. While the two traditions have much in common, they also have differences, but they, nevertheless, complement one another, each revealing in a different way the richness of the heritage of that great educational innovator and humanitarian, Edmund Rice.

NOTE

1. Since this article is intended for the general reader, I have tried to avoid too many references. The sources I have used are well known and include: Normoyle, MC, *A Tree is Planted* (1975, Christian Brothers, Dublin); Allen, D.H. *The Presentation Brothers*, Vol 1 (1993, Presentation Brothers, Cork).

MY FATHER SPOKE WITH SWANS
Patrick Galvin

I

Leaning on the parapet
Of the South Gate Bridge
My father spoke with swans
Remembering his days
With the Royal Munster Fusiliers.

India was dawn
The women cool
The sun cradled in his arms.
Sometimes,
When the clouds were wine
He washed his face in the Ganges.

The swans rose from the Lee
And held their wings.

II

Leaning on the mysteries
Of her twilight room
My mother spoke with God
Remembering Pearse
And the breath of Connolly.

Ireland was new
The men tall
The land mirrored their brightness.
Sometimes,
When the eagles called
She walked the roads to Bethlehem.

God opened his eyes
A loss for miracles.

III

From these two I was born
The Ganges swaying with the Lee
And gunfire rising to a fall.
My mother wore green till she died
My father died with swans.

Only the rivers remain
Slow bleeding.

PRESENTATION 2000

Frank J. Steele

I came to know the Presentation Brothers rather late in my life. I was never a pupil of theirs. I never taught with them. None of my children attended any of their schools. I was, in fact, almost forty before I spoke to a Presentation Brother. All my involvement up to then with muintearas Eamainn, with the household of Edmund Ignatius Rice, with the 'little flock' gathered in the Spirit around this 'Patriarch of the Monks of the West', had been via the Christian Brothers. As mentors and confrères, they had moulded me in all that pertained to the life and work of a religious educator through ten of the most formative years of my life. Yet I now seek to live as baptised, in the charism of Edmund, precisely as an Associate Member of the Presentation Congregation. A rough sketch of this vocational aspiration is my purpose here, and my particular reference will be, not to the past, but to the future, and, specifically, to the role of the Brothers in the coming years as facilitators of lay men and women, especially – though not exclusively – of those called, through, with and in Edmund, to the service of youth for the sake of the Gospel.

My interest in what for want of a better term I shall call 'association' with the Brothers derives from a search for a vision of life and a manner of living which, in the specific circumstances in which Providence has set me, will, through the grace of God, open me more and more to the presence and power of the Spirit – so that the logos uttered of me by the Father in the Son before time began will be made flesh; so that in my place and time I may be made Christ and Church for others; so that for the young, in particular, I may be made, in my words and in my deeds, herald of the Good News in the ministry of Christian formation; so that, in solidarity and community with men and women of like mind, intent and call, I may follow Christ in the footsteps of Edmund, in his household, and by means of the peculiar graces given by God to his people through this Rich Young Man who, as Christian, husband, father, Brother, did leave all to follow the Lord in the service of the young, in general, and of the poor, in particular.

To date my experience of 'Association' has centred especially on the monthly gathering at Mount St Joseph in Cork where, under the gentle but firm tutelage of Brother Clement, some ten of us meet to pray together, to ponder the Scriptures together, to consider together the increasing relevance of Edmund Rice in the actualisation of the values of the Gospel in the very many facets of our lives. This core experience has been augmented by engagement in common monthly Eucharistic celebration and devotion with a variety of groups clustered round Brother Matthew and the community in Mardyke House. Week-long courses, this year and last, deepening our understanding of personal development and of the person of Jesus respectively, for Brothers and Associates together, have both highlighted the actuality and adumbrated the potentiality of shared interests and aspirations. Occasional pilgrimages to Knock (the National Marian Shrine), to Callan (the birthplace of Edmund), to Mount Sion in Waterford (his burial-place), especially in conjunction with the Christian Brothers and their network of coadjutors, friends, supporters and benefactors, have served to give tangible manifestation to the widespread attraction of Edmund and to the mutuality of his followers in their various traditions. I have felt the hand of God at work in all of this and, through all of this, I have put my hand in his that he might lead me on.

However, I cannot help feeling that there is more to 'Association' than we have yet discerned and that this sense of something yet wanting is shared by Brothers and 'Associates' alike. As I, at least, see it – and I am expressing here no view but my own – we are now a mixture of prayer-group and study-group, an occasional, and still more or less chance, convergence of devotees of Edmund, of the Brothers, of their work. Through the enormous hospitality of the Brothers – through the zeal, competence and effectiveness of those who, like Brother Clement, guide our meetings; who, like Brother Bede, encourage participation and development; who, like Brother Stephen, courageously, imaginatively, perseveringly, supply leadership and formation – we have, as it were, a space in the hearts and in the homes of the Brothers, a local habitation and a name, as it were, a sense of togetherness and of belonging, a shared experience none of us, I believe, would ever wish to lose. It is precisely this sense of togetherness, the concomitant sense of the increasing richness of that which, as Brother and 'Associate', we hold together and share, that instils in us the further sense that we would, if we could, have more, even if we are not sure at all of the more we would have, even, indeed, if we are not sure we would not reject the more if we had it.

That which I, for one, would have, that, indeed, to which I feel called as to a 'vocation', is not so much association with, as incorporation in the Congregation. That which would seem to draw me is not some engagement that will speak to or for some part or aspect of my life, but, as I have indicated, a vision of life and a mode of living that will subsume my whole being and make of it – dare I say it – a whole burnt-offering, a sacrifice in spirit and in truth. I seek, in fact, a way of life that will facilitate the actualisation and expression of that to which I am called in the Sacrament of Baptism; that will do this in, through and for me as I am situated in the variety and complexity of my God-given state in life; and that will accomplish all of this, specifically and definitively, within the Household of Edmund. By ways and means as yet, admittedly, undetermined, this *modus vivendi* will root me as baptised in the charism of Edmund Rice; will bind me to his Brothers; will help me to recognise and realise the Paschal Mystery every day of my life – give me the wherewithal to live the dream of Jacob so that, amidst the hustle and bustle of home and school, amidst the hopes and fears of everyday experience, I may know and live this here and this now, whatever, whenever, wherever it may be, as nothing other than the House of God, the Gate of Heaven, as an opportunity to encounter the saving Presence of God at the heart of time and as a chance to rise in grace to be in that Presence forever in eternity; give me, too, that which I need to stride forward on a pilgrimage of faith, hope and love through the institutions, so that all the circumstances of human experience might be leavened, humanised, Christianised in and through the offer and acceptance of the Kingdom of God proclaimed and present in Christ Jesus.

In keeping with the charism of Edmund and the vocation of the Brothers, 'Association' – at least as I understand it – will serve especially the ministry of Christian formation. It will do this in all the circumstances in which youth is encountered, in the home, on the street, in the school, in the workplace. 'Association' will ensure that, in their pilgrimage, and in all its twists and turns, highs and lows, young people, particularly the marginalised amongst them, will have at their side and at their service, the Brothers themselves certainly, but right alongside the Brothers – formed by them, trained by them, sent by them, guided by them and empowered by them – men and women, parents, teachers, trainers, counsellors, mentors of all sorts and conditions, strong for the Kingdom, qualified in both personal and professional terms to explain and exemplify the Good News that is in Christ Jesus to the always-to-be-discovered and new-found land of youth.

This vision of 'Association' I see, not as a denial, but as a development of the vocation and traditions of the Brothers. Their way in the future will still be that of the service of youth for the sake of the Gospel. They will still retain, manage and teach their schools. They will continue to explore additional ways and means in the ministry of Christian formation. What is suggested here is that, amongst those new modes of Christian service provided by the Brothers, there will be that of sharing their vocation, their spirituality, their mission, especially the charism of Christian formation which they hold in trust from Edmund for the people of God, with their 'secular' brothers and sisters, of training themselves to train them to live the Gospel 'amid the bulks of actual things' and to proclaim it in the ministry of Christian formation by whatever means best suit their various and respective circumstances in life.

In purely human terms, it would be wholly understandable were the Brothers to conclude that they have neither the time nor the resources nor the personnel to take responsibility for this newfangled business of 'Association', so voracious in its demands, so nebulous in its origins, so uncertain in its outcome. However, from the very outset, Edmund taught his Brothers that 'the just man lives by faith'. Through the eyes of faith, this form of 'Association' – which, for a whole variety of reasons, is best regarded as one of a range of different forms of incorporation in, and/or co-operation with, the Congregation – will be seen to be prophetic in its responding convergence with the needs of Brothers, laity, and children at this time in the respective histories of the Congregation, of Ireland and of the Church itself. It is, in faith, a notion and an opportunity the time for which has come and, in accommodating which, the Brothers – who may not yet see wholly and clearly whom it is they have encountered on the way – are constraining the Pilgrim Christ to stay with them 'because it is towards evening and the day is now far spent'.

The Brothers may well feel that they have fished all night and caught nothing. In the faith of Edmund, let them push out into the deep and pay out their nets for, when to human eyes there seems little hope for any catch at all, it is precisely then that the Lord fills the nets even to breaking point. They must, of course, exercise the virtues and duties of prudence and discernment, but, in so doing, let theirs be the wisdom of Gamaliel who, in the face of something that was for him and his fellows both new and disturbing, advised that 'if this plan or this undertaking is of men, it will fail; but if it is of God, you will not be able to overthrow them'.

On the eve of the Third Millennium, in the Year of Edmund, like him, like Abraham, let us go forth together, Brother and 'Associate', from all that is known, familiar, and safe, to find the land which the Lord will give us if, in obedience to him, in charity towards each other, in service to the neighbour, we seek, in the heart of the Pilgrim Church, to tell our children what God has done to save his people.

THE TOPOLOGY OF SHELLS

On the death of my pupil James Dowdall who died in Paris
William Wall

The apparent movement in the spiral cortex
is Yeats's gyre calcifying. A world worn down
by the sea is a pebble rattling on a beach,
its dormant energy provoked by the ebb.

Dried wrack is scantling. You stood here
that August evening skimming stones,
each skip ramifying across the emptying ocean,
connecting us to the shore of that country

in one great ring, the stone at the core.
They will fly your coffin over those rings.
But which way does the gyre go inside the shell?
To spiral inward is to voyage down

the iridescent memory, backwards in time,
the world coiling into order, tapering to a place
so small & so intense that there's no release.
You'll have no luck that way. To go outwards

means losing touch, to swing loosely
at the world's rode while the strands unravel.
The frailest fibres hold you back.
The view is breathtaking. Do not be afraid.

God is somewhere in the chaos, an aimless boy
playing with knots & stones. When you throw
skimmers there you will see your coronae
amplify across the cosmos. Beyond that

is beyond our scope – the riding lights
stand so far out their loom will never
reach into our time. There is no other way.

PRESENTATION BROTHERS IN TRINIDAD AND TOBAGO

Anthony Lucky

The end of this year marks fifty years since the Presentation Brothers arrived in Trinidad and Tobago, their prime purpose being the establishment of Catholic secondary schools for young men.

Edmund Rice was born in Ireland in the second half of the eighteenth century and founded the Presentation and Christian Brothers in 1802. It is significant that in the fiftieth year of the Presentation presence in this country, Edmund Rice will be beatified in Rome.

In reminiscing about school days at Pres, San Fernando, almost every past student speaks in glowing terms of the Principal of his era. The Principal of one's era was always the best, yet the general consensus is that while each had his particular strengths his mission was the same as that of the others. Each strove to achieve and succeed in reaching his goal through imparting knowledge to the students. Education, religious and academic, and the good life were the common factors.

What impressed me at Pres, San Fernando, was the ability of the Brothers to create a thirst for knowledge, not only for subjects on the curriculum but for knowledge of Christ. The Brothers were educators but, first and foremost, they placed adherence to their religious vows.

Noticeable also was the ability of the Brothers to command respect without demanding it; to teach without dictating; to encourage and not discourage; to motivate and not demotivate. The teachers were able to mix education, sport and culture without one suffering at the expense of the other. Their prime concern was that we should always have God as our guide.

A spirit of togetherness existed. At school we were not just students but part of the family of Presentation. We were part of a Christian community and an extension of our own small communities, and our families.

Presentation College, San Fernando, has past students in every walk of life: priests, Brothers (two of whom are currently Principals in Trinidad, Brothers Michael Samuel and Benedict Taylor); two Prime Ministers, Cabinet Ministers, a Governor of the Central Bank, Supreme Court Judges and leaders in the private and public sectors. Last, but by no means least, are the many past students who are teachers at primary, secondary and tertiary level, who, I am confident, carry with them the emphasis in education that Edmund Rice loved.

It is the prayer of every past student that the hopes and aspirations of the Presentation and Christian Brothers, which are also those of their founder, Edmund Rice, will continue to be realised in new and ever-changing ways.

GREENMOUNT ORPHANAGE IN THE 1870s:
MEMORIES OF AN INMATE

Joseph A. Conroy

This little booklet,[1] with its meagre description of a few of the incidents that happened in old St Patrick's Orphanage, Greenmount, Cork, between the years 1871 and 1878, is not intended for public perusal, or as a literary production, as it is not expected that any person, excepting the boys themselves, would be interested in it, and because the writer has no literary aspirations. It is a work of a few hours, and was solely intended to take the place of the heart-to-heart talks that people often have of the days of their teens, but in this case, with no one to talk to, and the old boys scattered far and wide, the writer hopes it may fall in the way of some of them who will, no doubt, be pleased with these recollections of the days that are gone, and may bring them together again by correspondence or otherwise.

Cork: place of beauty and proverbial hospitality
There is no period in life as happy as childhood and no matter what its surroundings are, in either riches or poverty, memory will ever cling to these days of happy innocence with a fond recollection that time cannot destroy nor subsequent events efface. My boyhood days, like many others, had their alloy of suffering, principally because in my fourth year, with two younger brothers, I was left fatherless and nearly homeless, and had to depend on the kindness and charity of others for food and clothes. It was my good fortune, however, to be born in a city and county where hospitality is proverbial, and where the big-hearted people can never say no to the widow and orphan, and, though wealth and riches are not its share, there is more true charity there than in any other part of the world.

I am now speaking of Cork City, one of the prettiest places on the globe, and although it is forty years ago since I romped in its streets, and have since visited or lived in most of the large or celebrated cities of the world, yet for natural advantages, useful improvements, beautiful surroundings and a really delightful little city, give me Cork.

Death of father

I was born in 1864 in Cork City. Tragedy struck in my life when my father died in 1868 at the age of twenty-nine years. Such calamities can never be adequately provided against, and the Irish in those days had no money for insurance companies, if there were any, and the banks in Ireland were not overburdened with their deposits. I remember my father's funeral and the struggle my mother had to keep a home for us for some years afterwards.

I was sent early to school, first to the Christian Brothers on Blarney Lane, and occasionally I was sent on an errand to the Peacock Lane School, both perfect in their methods, but the lesson books were so expensive that I can yet see the sad face of my mother who could not afford the price of the new books needed whenever I was promoted.[2]

We lived in Duncan Street. Nearly opposite to our residence was St Peter's old Church and graveyard while, further south, was the Quaker Meeting-House, where William Penn held a religious service shortly before he started for America to form the community that was to bring about the State of Pennsylvania and its city of Philadelphia. There have always been close links between Cork and Philadelphia and the number of Corkonians who have settled and thrived there has been unusually high.

To Greenmount Orphanage

In my early years, the struggle for a home evidently over, I remember being taken to a Doctor O'Connor, on the quay near St Patrick's Bridge, who said I was a fine healthy little chap, and also to the Reverend Father James Fleming, who questioned me about my aunt etc. Afterward, with my aunt and mother, I recollect, as if it were yesterday, my first trip in a covered car up Barrack Street to Greenmount, to join the other boys in St Patrick's Orphanage. As we neared the gate of this truly Cork charity, a stone fight was in progress between the Bandon Road and the Lough Road boys. All the model tactics of the late Boer War were apparently anticipated and called into play by both

41

sides, and it was ended for the time being only by the appearance of great big Brother Joseph, from St Patrick's, with cane in hand, and, from the way they scattered, the boys had apparently had previous experience with him.

I feel sad now when I think of that first parting from my dear mother and kind aunt. It was one embrace after another, and their extreme sorrow then made me realise more than I can express now the change that had taken place in their lives, and, when I saw them for the first time leave me with strangers, I do not understand to this day how I got over it. When they did leave, however, Brother Joseph, who was in charge of the school, or home, talked nicely and kindly to me, and took me and introduced me to the other boys, also to my future teacher, Brother Patrick, and to their lay assistant, a Mr Bradley, whom the boys among themselves, in a spirit of kindness and affection, called 'Pat'.

The big buildings then in use are, no doubt, still there, the stone and mortar used being intended to last forever, and included two large dormitories, a refectory, kitchen, infirmary, day room, Brothers' rooms and parlours, all plain and neat and kept scrupulously clean by the boys and housekeepers then in charge.

The public or day school attached was in a large, high two-storey building near the public road, with two immense schoolrooms and classrooms, and with their high wooden panelled ceilings, large windows, and the outside stone stairways, they were healthy, safe and impressive, and fitted in every way for the school purposes of the Orphanage boys, and also the boys who came to day-school there.

Besides my many spells of homesickness, my anxious longing for a visit from my mother, and an attack of sore eyes that I had at this time, I am still able to remember the new lesson books I received, and the first time dear 'Pat' Bradley had us 'sing' the counties of Ulster – all are still fresh in my mind. For some reason I can never forget the reading lesson I then had: it was 'The Brook' with its attractive rhythm:

> For men may come and men may go,
> But I go on forever, etc.

Presentation Brothers take over management

I do not intend to dwell on the conditions that existed at St Patrick's in those days, as they were soon to be changed, the Brothers having only recently taken entire charge. Previously they had attended solely to the teaching, the housekeeping being looked after by 'Sully', as the boys called him, and his wife, with their assistants. At the time the school was over-crowded with boys intended for the new Industrial School, who were temporarily staying with us in the Orphanage. Sufficient to say that, before the Brothers' entrance, the place was run like most such institutions noted for their poor food and strict discipline (the rod system being in vogue) as if it were a crime to lose one's parents and be an orphan.

In a short time the Industrial boys were located in their own building, where Brothers Patrick and Augustine were in charge, and our Brother Joseph was sent during the day to teach in the Lancasterian School. In his place, Brother Baptist came with Brother Louis, and together they started the condition of things that made life worth living thereafter for the boys at St Patrick's.

Honour and house systems introduced

After Brother Baptist got thoroughly acquainted with each one of us, our history, our record, and our ability, he called us together one afternoon and announced, by the breaking of a rod in his hand, that the punishment system had ended at Greenmount and that from now on the boys would be ruled by the merit system, and that honour would be exacted from each one of us, and that boys too bad to be with us would be sent elsewhere.

There were fifty boys in the place, ranging in age from eight to fourteen or fifteen years, all well-developed, healthy lads. Brother Baptist first divided us into four classes by asking us to select four class leaders, or monitors, by ballot, who in turn picked twelve boys, one at a time, for whom they were to be responsible, and to these monitors the boys were to look for first aid and advice. It was very interesting and keenly appreciated by the Brothers and the boys.

Four class leaders

The first four boys elected were known to us principally by their nicknames, which I will use hereafter. There were Bell, Mull, Matt and Gus, and their election accorded them special privileges at the table and different clothes from the other boys, an arrangement which made them feel their responsibility and take an interest in the boys of their selection, and who had elected them.

Bell was known amongst us as the literary or smart boy of the school and in the book line he had no equal. Mull was a big, strong, brave boy, with little taste for learning, and a great love of work, and he had the confidence of everyone when it was a question of strength or nerve. Matt was the idol of the school, and the confidant and banker of the other boys. He was both religious and good, and was devoted to his prayers and church, but, at the same time, was well up in his lessons, and gave trouble to no one. Gus was Master of Ceremonies at all the affairs that took place in the school. He also played the harmonium in the church, and sang in solo or read the addresses which we sometimes presented to important persons. He was the one sent on special errands, was a good cricket player, as well as in other games, was generous with the boys, and was well liked and popular with them. No selection could have been better.

Extra-curricular activities

With this foundation Brother Baptist further announced that we were to have a library, a chemical laboratory, a band, a singing class, drawing lessons, a drill master, lessons in elocution, with periodical plays. He also purchased for us a small, foot-powered printing press, with sufficient type to print a small four-page paper, which we got out occasionally. Bell was editor-in-chief of this production, and when it appeared everyone was pleased, and the advertisements procured helped to make it profitable as well as instructive.

The library and bookcase were the gifts of Mayor Penrose, and were a source of great pleasure and help to the boys, and the hunting tales of America by Cooper, with Schmidt's and Conscience's tales, were so popular that we had to wait our turn for these books.

Our drawing lessons were supplemented with water colours, and it would surprise you to see the pretty 'Patrick Crosses', chalices and other things the boys drew and painted. Mr Sargeant was the music teacher at the time and the great pains he took to teach part-singing enabled him to have a class that was a credit to the school. The choir was well trained and the Masses we sang were up to a very high standard.

We had an excellent drill master and the drill helped us in health as well as in appearance. Mr Bradley was the elocutionist of the school and the boys were always interested when he recited for us 'Robert of Sicily' or 'The Heart Bowed Down' etc.

Brother Baptist also produced plays such as *Box and Cox* and *The Village Lawyer*, Bell, Mull and Gus taking the leading parts and, between the acts, I remember that Bell recited 'Rienzi to the Romans', while Gus and another boy sang 'Oh, Give to Me those Early Flowers' and 'How the Wind is Blowing', both great songs in those days. These play nights were famous: we usually had the Bishop, many priests, the Mayor and Aldermen, the patrons of the school and their friends, and, after the play, they were entertained with refreshments, while the boys had a feast of candy, fruit and cakes, and, of course, our band finished with music.

Band and excursions

The band was first a fife and drum corps and later a brass band of twenty pieces. It was a great attraction for the boys within and without the school, although it was hard work out of fifty boys, and all young, to keep up such a band, but with twenty players, and a young substitute learning each instrument, we kept nearly the whole school interested. We had no band when I was admitted. The former boys had all left, but their old instruments of fifes and drums were still there.

One Sunday, when some of these older boys paid us a visit, they put on the drums and got the fifes tuned up and started 'Nellie Gray' and other airs then up-to-date, and then our whole desire was to have a band, and Brother Baptist got it for us. First a fife and drum corps, and when we did so well with that he interested several well-known men who gave us the brass band and it was not long before we could play 'God Save Ireland',

'Adeste Fidelis' and 'Silver Threads among the Gold' etc.

The band was all right. I have since heard Sousa and Gilmore and other artists, but they have never appealed to me like the marches that we got out of these instruments in bygone days. Our band also helped to entertain the boys during our many excursions. Father Tom and Brother Baptist were a team who loved the boys and had us on many excursions down the river, once, I remember, with the gas house employees, and often to Crosshaven and Aghada, and other nice places nearer the sea, where we had a good time and plenty to eat. I hope the band still plays and the boys still have the same summer outings.

Menu problems solved

One of the great problems Brother Baptist found was to keep the boys well fed. Good food would do it, but fifty boys had fifty different tastes. What you like, if little, does you more good than disagreeable quantity, so we had generous old Denis Lucey, the grocer, and one of the Directors and Doctor Cremin, a real kind man, Father James Fleming and Father Tom Fleming, both kindness and goodness personified, and some others come to the school and examine what we were getting to eat and suggest within reason and within the means of the school the best for us. After some talk all agreed to give the boys a chance to suggest something and, with modifications, their ideas were adopted at a saving in the expense account of the school, doctor's bills and health, and with satisfaction to everyone.

As nearly as I can remember, we got well-cooked oatmeal, with milk and sugar, and plenty of bread and American apple-butter, and properly made tea for breakfast, with eggs on Sundays or holidays, cooked in some palatable way. For supper we had cooked fruit of some kind, plenty of bread, good milk or cocoa. At twelve o'clock each day Brother Baptist introduced a lunch, giving the boys cakes or buns supplied very reasonably by Albert bakery and this broke the long fast from breakfast right to dinner at three and made our school day more pleasant.

The Directors were surprised that he (Brother Baptist) was able to do apparently so much with an actual decrease in expense, but he was a great manager, and the Donation Day he established on June 24th each year for visitors simply loaded the school with presents of good clothes, fruit, etc. and was altogether a great success. In those days the band played all day for the visitors, and it appeared to me that it made everyone happy and anxious to give and help him. He also doubled the number of annual subscribers at that time, and the annual charity sermon that we listened to each November from the altar steps of St Finbarr's, dressed in our new clothes, became more popular each year.

Brother Baptist took an interest in everything. He had a brother a physician, and, from him, he obtained simple remedies and first aids for sickness, etc. which he used to apply very often, and he also had the doctor give us lessons in keeping well, cleaning our teeth, regular habits, chewing our food properly, and such matters, that we have never forgotten, and it would have surprised many to see Brother Baptist taste the food each day that we received, and once I remember he said the tea was boiled into poison, and had it all thrown out and made us wait until fresh tea could be properly brewed.

Novena to St Joseph: Mr Leahy answers

No one must think for a moment that spiritual things were forgotten in St Patrick's, far from it. We had our chapel and daily mass, which Gus served each morning and I shall never forget the first time he served for Father Tom Fleming as the latter announced that poor Gus' responses were in 'bog' Latin.

Monthly confession and communion was the rule and novenas and morning and evening prayers were regular. I guess that Brother Joseph remembers yet the novena we made one time to St Joseph for help to pay off the debt that threatened the school, when in the midst of it, most providentially, Mr D. F. Leahy of Shanakiel House, met the chaplain, Father James Fleming, and asked him how the school was getting on and, on being told of the debt, said, 'I will pay it off'. And he did so that same day, and with tears in his eyes good Brother Joseph told us boys of it that night before the altar, and you can rest assured that we said the prayers then all right, for who could doubt that St Joseph heard us?

Among the religious papers and books we received was the *Ave Maria* from America which was always a welcome one in the school and I still read it, and, while the cover has changed, the good words in it are still the same. All through the building were statues and pious pictures, and we all wore scapulars, and had our beads and prayerbooks, and to give an example of how good some of the boys were, I will relate a few years of Matt's life and his pious death, for if ever there was a saint in the calendar, Matt was one.

Story of saintly boy, Matt

Matt, as I said before, was a monitor or class leader. He was the boy's banker, gentle, loving and kind, trusted by everyone, faithful and honest, and he never said a dirty or unchaste word, or listened to any bad talk. Matt's mother was living and was a Protestant, as was his stepfather. They were both very good people, but truly wedded to their faith, and both loved Matt and he loved them, but he could not accept their religion, and it was under his father's will that he had to remain in the school until he was fifteen years of age, and that time was then fast approaching. The boys used to ask him if, when he left, he would give up his old church and faith for his mother's and the fervour and piety of his answer would convince anyone of his sincerity.

Matt had a little room of his own as store-keeper under the stairway in the new building, and in it he had a little altar to the Blessed Mother, with candles and flowers, and many minutes he spent there in prayer. Under it he kept our bank money, and never was it touched, as Matt and the Blessed Mother were, to our minds, the keepers, and no boy would dare molest or disturb it – we loved them both too well.

I could fill a volume with the many good works and deeds of that dear, good boy, who, with all his purity and goodness, was a leader in field sports and in his lessons and never received a bad mark for any inattention in either.

Matt was to leave us on the first of July 1877. He knew it, we knew it and he disliked to go. With the other three monitors mentioned, he slept in the end of the old dormitory, and one night in May he woke one of them up to say that he was spitting all night and he was weak but hat he had no pain, merely a choking feeling, but, when daylight came, we found it was blood, and the next day the doctor pronounced it a lung haemorrhage and poor Matt went to the infirmary at once, on the same floor, and never left it alive.

I never saw anyone so patient, resigned and happy – even anxious – to go to his reward. His first anxiety was to keep his little altar in shape and we boys did it for him, for we loved it for his sake, if nothing else. We all visited him from time to time and brought him flowers, etc. and the new altar that Brother Baptist placed in his room pleased him very much. Some of the priests came to see him and also the other Brothers, including the Superior, Brother Austin, and at night he asked me and the other boys to say the Rosary with him and light the candles on the altar in his room.

The Trustees, Brothers and boys were all deeply affected by the illness of poor Matt and his parents were heart-broken. We all knew that he could not live and he knew it and it was pathetic to hear him say that he was never going to change his faith – and he never did. He died in it the death of a saint.

During the last three days of June 1877, Father Tom Reilly was conducting a Triduum in honour of the Sacred Heart and on the last day of June, after the evening exercises and benediction, he was summoned to Matt's room and brought with him the Blessed Sacrament in procession and I had to run to the South Monastery for an indulgenced crucifix Brother Austin had, and, with this clasped in his hands, and after receiving his last holy communion, and saying the prayers for the dying with us, poor Matt, amid the prayers and tears of all present, passed away, as much a saint as ever lived, on the eve of the day his parents would have claimed him from us.

There were many other good boys in the school and the Brothers never had better pupils in piety than the boys in the 1870s in Greenmount.

*

Sport and games

In games and at play the boys were the equal of any in the neighbourhood. The Bluecoat School boys, under Dr Webster, were religious and national enemies of ours, as we thought, but one day Father Tom Reilly and Dr Webster got together and made us boys all the better friends, and many a game of cricket we played together after that. Only once did the Bluecoats beat us. The champion of our school was Gus, who on six occasions 'carried the bat'. Even Father Tom, no mean bowler, tried to put him out, and Brother Baptist also failed at it. Gus was also a good handball player and Brother Baptist enjoyed a game with him immensely.

Football was introduced by Father James Fleming, who one day visited us and had with him a brand new ball, and the first kick he gave it on the green opposite the school started ball playing, and after that we had many games. Brother Louis and Brother Baptist were often captains of the opposing teams, and the cyclonic strength of Brother Louis was well matched in the fleet and shifty ways of Brother Baptist.

Fishing and drama at the Lough

Fishing was another amusement with us, and with rod and line we spent many hours around the Lough looking for goldfish, and those of us who did not fish made boats. Brother Joseph was a son of the sea and taught us how to rig them. It was on one of these occasions that a beautifully built model brig was caught in the weeds in the deep portion of the Lough and one of the boys went out, in a long foot-washing box we had, to save it. In some way it leaked and got caught also and the boy was sinking in the deep water about two hundred yards from shore when Brother Joseph tore off some gates, strapped them together, and, with a shovel, paddled out only to be likewise caught. Their danger was imminent and the excitement high. The police were called and the chilly waters were weakening both, when Mull, the strong and brave boy of the school, ran all the way to the slip at the foot of Barrack Street and, without asking anyone to help him, put a boat with two oars on a waggon and had the driver bring it to the Lough and in thirty minutes was rowing out to Brother Joseph and the boy, thereby saving both their lives. The newspapers next day gave him great praise and credit and he really deserved it.

This was not the first time Brother Joseph risked his life to save boys. Some time previous to this event, in a hole in the Lee, near the weir, at the waterworks, he plunged fully-dressed into thirty feet of water and saved from death one of our boys, Sammy Davis, sinking the third time. Other Brothers in the school were also equally brave and I remember having heard that Brother Regis, Brother John and Brother Louis all took risks in the same way at Pike Hole and the Beardyman's Hole on the Lee, but outside of these places, the boys had very safe bathing at Sandy's Mills and along the coast and on the Lee near the waterworks and I assure you that we all enjoyed it very much.

Pets and pastimes

Among many other outdoor pastimes we gathered wild flowers, bees, etc. The Brothers gave us little garden plots around the yards to cultivate and we planted them with the wild flowers that we gathered and we built nests or hives there for the bees and were delighted to see these bees leaving and returning to them. The Brothers became so interested that later they built an elaborate apiary for honey bees and their industry was a great lesson to us, not to speak of the additional exercise we had in caring for the flowers and trees – all entertaining as well as healthful.

Pets and domestic animals were also introduced and Mr Lucey, already mentioned, allowed us the use of his drying field where we soon had many chickens and ducks, thereby getting enough eggs to supply us all the time. Mull, with his farm ideas, had some little pigs purchased, and, with his care and attention outside of school hours, they were soon big and strong and were sold at a handsome profit and the number always increasing to advantage. We also had some rabbits and several pigeons and I cannot forget the jackdaw that would follow us to school and church and table and several times insisted on sleeping in the dormitory. All these pets made us kind to animals and taught us that kindness is the foundation of friendship. About that time Dean Murphy gave Father Tom Fleming 'Tip' and 'Jet', two famous little dogs, and it is needless to say that they got so attached to us boys that you were very likely to find them in chapel or school or wherever we were.

Brother Baptist brought out the best in boys

The greatest good Brother Baptist accomplished was the manly, truthful and generous disposition he imbued in the boys. The monitor arrangement, the honour and four-class system were elegant and the rewards he gave each class where the average merits of over half of the boys were up to standard were grand indeed and made each class work together and made each boy in it take an interest in his fellow students.

The doors and walls were no longer necessary to keep us in – in fact, they were only of use in keeping unwelcome people out. You will hardly believe it, but, poor as we were, one night two robbers broke in and were about to ransack the chapel and had rifled the Brothers' parlour, when they were discovered by Bell, who was waiting on a sick boy in his class and in a few minutes the four monitors were all dressed and had quietly alarmed the Brothers and, with pokers and sticks, they captured two English sailors who fought with knives before they were subdued. The bravery of the four monitors on this occasion was highly praised by the judge before whom these men were brought and by the Brothers who witnessed it.

It became current talk in Cork that there were no better boys than the Greenmount lads, and this liberty got us used to the city and prepared us for after life and also led the way to a new idea which had just started about the time I left there. It worked well then and I am told is working now there and in other large cities.

Part-time jobs

Brother Baptist had a faculty of allowing the boys to choose a little for themselves and when, one day, one of the large stores became interested in one of the boys sent on an errand and offered him a position for a few hours daily, with the privilege of still living in the school and continuing his studies, it opened up a new line of thought for Brother Baptist. Very shortly after that we had ten boys employed in various places – office boys, one a baker, another a printer, one in a dry goods store, another in a grocery store, etc., all returning each evening to the school and bringing their weekly wages to Brother Baptist.

The other boys in the school were allowed to follow as much as possible their natural bent and, as a result, we had barbers and a good tailor among them, although we were all taught how to sew and mend our clothes and, at inspection each morning at 8.45, there was trouble if any dirty or broken shoes, unclean hands or faces or other things that could be remedied were discovered. We also had a good shoemaker, a painter or two, a gardener, sacristan, organist, cooks, and, in fact, we were all taught to be handy men as much as possible.

Storytellers
Dark, long winter evenings were varied with reading and games, all generously supplied by the Brothers. Concerts and recitations we often had, but what we enjoyed most was story-telling, and you have missed something if you never heard Brother Joseph tell of 'The Siege of Granada' and the war between the Moors and Spaniards, including the heroism of the many Irishmen he wove into it for the boys. Among the older boys were also many good story-tellers and the best was, I think, Watty, as he was known among his chums. He was the best read and best behaved in the older set or class and beloved by all his teachers – and, in fact, all of us. So much so that once when he had typhoid fever, and it was thought that he would die, the gloom was great throughout the school and, as I had to do a little waiting on him, I was constantly asked how he was, and when he requested an orange on one occasion, and they were hard to get, I was sent all around Cork City until I bought some that just arrived, and the gladness it created when I arrived with them showed the real love and affection for Watty, the storyteller.

Supportive religious atmosphere
Our boys were always the leaders in examinations for first holy communion and confirmation and the Bishop and priests and Brothers were proud of us when, year after year, not one was refused admission to these sacraments – we were experts in our catechism.

Father Tom Fleming heard my first confession and gave me first holy communion, and Father Joseph Fleming was my sponsor when confirmed by Bishop Delaney, that good friend of the boys, in the parish chapel, as we called it, of St Finbarr's. Both of these happy events are distinctly clear in my memory and preparation for holy communion, including my general confession, new clothes, silence, and seclusion the night before, made me reverence that great event in a way never to be forgotten.

On the day of it, after holy mass and a long, fervent thanksgiving, the Brothers gave us an elaborate breakfast, and after it presents of beads and prayer books, and we were then given liberty to romp free in the woods all day until five p.m. with sufficient money to get a good lunch at any place we might select. We were also exempt from study and made to feel that it was an epoch in the journey of our existence and that man does not live, with or without the faith, who does not feel happy in recollecting the innocence and joy he felt on that long gone day – full of faith and confidence in the God who made him.

Holy confirmation was just as elaborate in preparation, but being older boys then, we were more serious and it impressed us in a different way. Responsibility was taught to us then and as soldiers, we were expected to show by word and example our training and our faith – never to be ashamed to own up to it, and better still, never to do anything to disgrace it. May God bless Father Tom and Father James for their kindness. These were surely glorious days.

Sincere thanks

Where are all these dear Brothers who helped us then and the bright good lads who were so happy together? We, as boys or men, should never forget the good Brothers who, though in no way related to us, for the love of God gave up their lives to make us happy and to teach us what we needed to become useful men, and we should, when able, show our appreciation in the many ways we know that can help them. As one of the boys of the 1870s, I certainly thank the good Brothers for all I am and have.

NOTES

1. This is the text, with some omissions and slight editing, of the booklet. *Greenmount in the Seventies* by Kingwith, *The nom de plume* used by Joseph A. Conroy, and printed by Todd Printing Co., 2317 Colombia Ave, Philadelphia. Though there is no publication date listed, we can assume it was published about 1910 because its successor, *With the Monks*, was printed by the same firm and published in 1911.

   The author's full name was Joseph Augustine Conroy, born at 50 Duncan (now Grattan) Street, Cork. Though he states in this booklet that he was born in 1864, there is a baptismal record for him in SS Peter and Paul Church, Cork, confirming that he was baptised there by Rev. Jeremiah Twomey PP on 6 September, 1863, having been born on 29 August the same year. His mother was Margaret Foley and his father Joseph Conroy, a carver and member of Cork Mechanics' Provident Society. Research in Cork archives confirms all the facts mentioned in the booklet.

   After completing his schooling in Greenmount in 1878, Mr Conroy went to live with the Presentation Brother in the South Monastery, Douglas Street, Cork, with the idea of later becoming a member. He began teaching in the South Monastery school as a monitor in 1878, continuing to live with the Brothers for the following three years. Initially he was successful as a teacher in the junior classes but encountered some difficulties in 'Fourth Class'. With a view to restoring his confidence, the Brothers arranged a transfer for him to the Lancasterian School in Washington Street, Cork, but here too he became discouraged by his teaching performance and gradually became convinced that he was not destined to be a teacher, and, consequently, not a Presentation Brothers either. He remained very attached to the Brothers, however, and they secured employment for him at the Patrician Academy, Mallow. Later, he went to Dublin to work in a pharmacy and from there to Youghal where he worked as a book-keeper in a grocery store before emigrating to Philadelphia. The story of Conroy's life after leaving Greenmount is dealt with in his booklet, *With the Monks* (Philadelphia, 1911). There are copies of eight of Conroy's booklets in the archives of Presentation Brothers, Mount St Joseph, Cork, including *Christmas Eve, Neighbours, The Bells, Ned Willis, I Will Arise, Matt Murphy, Greenmount in the Seventies, With the Monks.* His purpose in writing these booklets, all published at his own expense, seemed to be twofold: to express gratitude and appreciation to the Presentation Brothers for their loving care of him in his youth and to carry on their mission of Christian education, in his own modest way, through the written word. See J. Collins, *Presentation Studies,* 1990, No. 7, 16.

2. The Christian Brothers withdrew their affiliation with the National Board of Education in 1836. This meant the loss of capitation grants and of school textbooks published by the Board and supplied at cost price. While the Christian Brothers published their own textbooks to meet their needs the cost of these far exceeded the cost of the schoolbooks of the Board. Since the Presentation Brothers, on the other hand, maintained their affiliation with the Board, they were able to supply their pupils with schoolbooks at a much lower cost.

3. Some people mentioned:
Bishop Delaney: William Delaney (1804-86), Bishop of Cork 1848-86
Brother Baptist: Thomas Baptist Moloney (1843-1910). Entered Presentation Brothers, Cork, 1863.
Brother Joseph: Jeremiah Joseph O'Callaghan (1841-1915). Entered Presentation Brothers, Cork, 1856.
Brother Patrick: William Patrick Shine (1843-1905). Entered Presentation Brothers, Cork, 1868.
Brother Augustine Ryan (b.c.1848. Left Presentation Brothers 1880s)
Brother Louis: Cornelius Louis O'Mullane (1857-1902). Entered Presentation Brothers, Cork, 1881.
Father Tom Fleming: Ordained 1871.
Father James Fleming: Ordained 1865.

NOTHING IS SAFE
Patrick Galvin

Nothing is safe anymore.
I wrote a poem last night
And when I woke up this morning
There was no sign of it.

I thought the mice had eaten it
(We're subject to mice in this house)
But then again
Why should they?
Poetry doesn't agree with mice.

Of course,
The present climate being
What it is
Anything may have happened –
A sudden rainstorm
During the night
The cold air
Thieving through the window
And the poem dies of pneumonia.

Next time I write a poem
I'll send it to my aunt
Who lives in a madhouse.
She's blind
But she likes the texture of paper.
She hods it in her hand
Crinkles it up
And listens to the sound.

Perhaps
That's all that matters
In the end –
The sound of paper
Screaming in the hand.

BROTHER PAUL TOWNSEND: EXEMPLAR OF THE PRESENTATION TRADITION

J. Matthew Feheney FPM

Brother Edmund Paul Townsend was a key figure in the history of the Presentation Brothers during the nineteenth century. Not only was he one of the first companions of Brother Michael Augustine Riordan in the new Presentation Monastery in Douglas Street, Cork, but he was also the latter's successor as superior of the mother house there. Moreover, he was also the founder of the second and third schools of the Presentation Brothers, in Killarney and Milltown respectively. Later, in Cork, he was one of the most highly respected and esteemed members of his Congregation and of the teaching profession as a whole.

But, arguably, even more interesting than these achievements is his evidence before the Powis Commission of Inquiry into Primary Schooling in Ireland in 1868, when he outlined, albeit briefly, his ideas on certain aspects of education. These ideas, it is reasonable to assume, were, to a large extent, shared by his confrères in the embryonic Congregation of the Presentation Brothers. He could, therefore, be regarded as outlining a tentative – and surprisingly broad-minded – Presentation philosophy of education. (Powis, pp. 758-60)

Early years

Edmund Townsend was born in the barony of Duhallow, Co Cork, in 1798. Though no details have survived about his own immediate family, there was a belief, widespread among his pupils and past pupils, that he was a scion of a noble house and a Protestant before his entry to the Presentation Brothers. It is possible that he may have been a convert from Protestantism because, as Allen points out, there were several Protestant families of that surname in the barony at the time. Moreover, the writer of the annals in the Presentation monastery, Milltown, one of the houses he founded, hints at this also:

In a time when university education was the exclusive privilege of the Protestant minority, Brother Paul received an
education equal to that afforded by present-day universi-
ties. He could speak four languages – Irish, English,
French and German, and was as well a famous mathemati-
cian. He became an architect, but soon abandoned a lucra-
tive profession, to become a monk, a criminal in the eyes
of the law. (Allen, 43)

It is not suggested, however, that Brother Paul did actually attend
Trinity College, Dublin, the only university in Ireland at the
time, but that he did attend some school of further education. In
fact, little is known of Brother Paul's early education, though the
writer of his obituary notice (not the same as the Milltown annalist), who knew him well, says that he had trained as an architect,
and was proficient in mathematics, as well as in French, German
and Irish. While it is probable that he acquired his training in
architecture through apprenticeship to a practising architect, it is
more difficult to surmise where he received his general education,
especially the two foreign languages with which he is credited.

Since both were architects, it probably that he had some association with Brother Michael Augustine Riordan before the autumn
of 1826, at which time the latter left the North Monastery, Cork,
to set up a foundation in the South Parish. Though we are not
sure of this, we do know that, as a mature man of twenty-nine
years, he was one of Brother Riordan's assistants in the school
which opened in temporary accommodation in a disused corn
store in Cat Lane, off Barrack Street, Cork, on 1 July 1827. This
school moved to new premises in the South Monastery, Douglas
Street, Cork, built by Brother Riordan, in 1829.

Like Edmund Rice, Paul had been contemplating another
form of religious life before he met Brother Riordan and became
attracted to the latter's educational work for poor children. But,
whereas Edmund Rice's first attraction was towards the
Augustinians, Paul's was towards the Cistercians. In the work of
education, however, Paul found his true vocation. He was not
long with Brother Riordan before he became indispensable, his
many talents, striking personality and great personal charm mak-

ing him an ideal assistant. Paul also had another characteristic in common with Edmund Rice. This was his baptismal name: though baptised Edmund, he chose the name Paul on entering the Presentation Brothers to signify his adoption of a new way of life.

By 1838 Paul was assistant to Brother Riordan in the South Monastery and acting head of the Lancasterian School in Cork, of which Brother Riordan was superintendent, when, at the request of Bishop Egan of Kerry, he went, with three companions, to open a school in Killarney. Here the community had to endure unusual poverty and hardship, all four being compelled to sleep in one room about twelve feet square, and this even when one suffered a severe illness and another died of typhus.

The school in Killarney prospered, however, under Paul's guidance, even though the buildings were inadequate and unsuitable. It was a measure of the Bishop's satisfaction with the work of the Brothers in Killarney that, in 1842, he invited Paul to open another school in the diocese, this time in Milltown, about ten miles west of Killarney. This invitation Paul gladly accepted. He had first, however, to build the new school. Here he used his training and experience as an architect and engaged local workmen to quarry the stone, after which he supervised the building of the monastery and schoolrooms. On completion of the school in Milltown, he was commissioned by the Bishop of Kerry to build a new monastery and school in Killarney. This necessitated his return from Milltown to Killarney.

Though Paul, as someone with architectural training, was capable of drawing up a plan for the new school in Killarney, the Bishop felt that Pugin, who was designing the new neo-Gothic cathedral for the town, should be involved. Paul agreed and Pugin submitted a plan based on that of the nearby ancient ruin of Muckross Abbey, with a cloister in the centre of the building. Like many of Pugin's famous designs, only a sketch plan was supplied. Though the design was extremely attractive, Paul was left to pay the forty guineas which the great Augustus Welby charged for his services, the Bishop having deftly side-stepped paying the bill. Incidentally, the forty guineas was equivalent to one third of the entire annual income of the community at the time.

Before the new monastery and school in Killarney could be completed, however, the terrible tragedy of the Great Famine struck Ireland, affecting Kerry no less than other parts of the country. The money to build the new school in Killarney had to be raised by collections of various kinds, and such fund-raising proved impractical, if not unthinkable, during the famine years when every available penny had to be used to provide meals for the children. As things developed, therefore, it fell to Paul's successor to complete the fine cut-stone building designed by Pugin to complement the magnificent Cathedral nearby.

Paul did, however, work hard to obtain a choice site for the new monastery and school in Killarney. This was known as Falvey's 'Inch' and was donated by Mrs Raymond, a great benefactor of the school. Though the site, amounting to five acres, was the legal property of Mrs Raymond, it was being used by some local people who put obstacles in the way of Paul taking possession of it. Eventually, he had to have recourse to the law courts to get possession of the site and the tiresome legal proceedings were a source of great irritation to him. On top of this, no sooner had he taken possession of the ground than the Bishop requested part of it as a site for Pugin's new Cathedral. Though Paul was quite willing to donate a site for the Cathedral, he insisted on a separate, independent entrance to the monastery and school and this entailed more lengthy negotiations.

Return to Cork

In 1846, the health of Brother Augustine Riordan, the superior of the mother house in Cork, began to decline and the Cork community requested Paul's return from Killarney. Bishop Egan, however, declined to permit him to return on the grounds that he was indispensable. Finally, when Brother Augustine died in Cork in January 1848 and Paul was nominated by the Cork community to succeed him as Superior, Dr Egan relented, most probably in return for a promise from Paul to send him some Brothers from Cork.

The post of Superior in Cork included responsibility for superintending both the South Monastery School and the larger Lancasterian School in Great George Street, now the Western

Road, Cork, which had an enrolment of about eight hundred pupils. It is with this latter school especially that he was popularly associated as the years went on. He continued as Superior in the South Monastery, Douglas Street, and as Manager of these two schools, until bodily infirmity forced him to retire in 1871 at the age of seventy-three.

Paul builds Greenmount School

In 1854, Paul began building the Greenmount National School. The site was the old Gallows Green, a low hill close to St Finbarr's (Church of Ireland) Cathedral, for which he obtained a five hundred year lease from Cork City Corporation at an annual rent equivalent to £1.50. Gallows Green was the site of public executions in Cork, and, to get away from its unpleasant associations, he renamed the place Greenmount, a name which it has retained ever since. He explained his reasons for opening this school to the Powis Commission in 1868:

> We thought it better to build a school and take it to the poor bare-footed children, rather than have them coming to us. We thought we could be better able to travel to them, being well shod and clothed, than have the poor children coming to us. We wished to accommodate the children and built this school at an expense of about £2,000. (Powis, Q.17, 286)

The Annals of the South Monastery describe the difficulties Paul and his companions overcame in raising the money and getting the building erected:

> He was his own architect and clerk of works and direct labour was employed. He taught in the old Lancasterian School every day, and in the evenings and on Saturdays he begged the money in Cork city, to pay his tradesmen and labourers on Saturday evening. (Allen, 155)

Paul as an architect

Though the annalist of the South Monastery is emphatic that

Paul trained as an architect, unlike Brother Riordan, architecture played a very minor part in his life after he entered the Presentation Brothers. Paul is on record as building only two schools: that in Milltown, County Kerry, begun in 1842, and the National School, Greenmount, Cork, in 1854. Though he also laid the foundations of the monastery and school in Killarney in 1846, the Great Famine and shortage of money brought this project to a standstill for several years. Paul's involvement in architecture after joining the Presentation Brothers seemed to be motivated solely by the needs in hand rather than a desire for self-fulfilment. When a school had to be built, he went to his drawing board and got on with the job. Once the school was built, however, he reverted to his normal work as teacher or director of schools.

The involvement in architecture of Paul's mentor and superior, Brother Michael Augustine Riordan, was, however, much more intense and continuous. As long as Bishop Murphy was alive, he never seemed to escape from his original profession. His continued involvement in church architecture has been discussed elsewhere in this volume (Feheney, 'Edmund Rice and the Presentation Brothers'). Suffice it to say here that he was believed to be the architect of many of the churches built in the dioceses of Cork, Ross and Cloyne in the first half of the nineteenth century. From what we know of Brother Riordan, however, it is more likely that this involvement in building churches was due to pressure from his friend, patron and religious superior, Bishop John Murphy, than to his own personal need for self-fulfilment or involvement in a field of endeavour other than education.

Paul, on the other hand, never became involved in diocesan affairs, church building or otherwise. All his time and energy were devoted to his community, schools and pupils. He was meticulous in keeping records and the financial transactions of the South Monastery for the period, in his fine, bold handwriting, are preserved in the archives of the Presentation Brothers.

Long association with the 'Lancs'
Paul enjoyed enormous respect and esteem as Director of the Lancasterian School in Cork, popularly known as the Lancs. The school was set up in 1814 along the lines advocated by Reverend

Joseph Lancaster in England. Though Reverend Alexander Bell devised a similar system, whereby a large number of children were taught by a small number of teachers, using student-teachers or monitors to help in the instruction, the Catholic Church preferred Lancaster's method mainly because his system was devised for non-conformists whereas Bell's was a Church of England system. Brother Riordan and the Presentation Brothers were invited by the Cork Charitable Society, Managers of the school, to assume responsibility for the administration and staffing of this historic institution in 1829.

A past pupil of this school describes Brother Paul as follows:

> Brother Paul was an ideal gentleman, in his deportment, in his carriage, and in his manner; he was most affable and courteous to everybody; he spoke with a tone of sincerity in everything he said, and his kindness of heart and innate nobility of character won him the respect and admiration of all. He had great affection for children and naturally enough was loved and venerated by them in return...It was most edifying to hear him say the prayers with the boys in the school with much unction and fervour, and to listen to his religious instruction in the afternoon, to the advanced pupils in the Lecture Room, was a real treat in itself. The force he put into these instructions has never been forgotten and I firmly believe that the words which he uttered with such sincerity and ardour never fell on deaf ears. (Allen, 145)

Paul was remarkable for the courteousness, charm, kindness and good humour which were characteristic of him. In addition to being known as Brother Paul, he was sometimes affectionately called Father Paul and yet, at other times he was formally addressed as Mr Townsend. The word 'gentleman' was also frequently used to describe him. One past pupil wrote:

> I doubt if ever a teacher of youth was more esteemed, admired and loved better than Father Paul was by the boys who had the good luck to be catered for intellectually by

him. He stood with the boys for something more than a schoolmaster. He was not feared, any more than a loving father may be said to be feared, for we felt that he was sympathetic, just, considerate and gave us of his best. He seemed to me at the time to belong to the past, he was so courtly in his demeanour... In or out of school, he carried a perpetual smile ... The bigger boys and monitors almost adored him. (Feheney, 11)

He showed the same courtesy towards parents and exercised the same charm over them. The same past pupil described Paul's reception of himself and his mother in the Lancasterian School:

Mother took me to the Lancs. one Monday morning, where she had an interview with Father Paul, who received her, as was his wont, with great affability. Mother was charmed with him and her admiration lasted throughout her lifetime. (Feheney, 11)

Attitude towards Fenian nationalism

Paul lived through the period of intense nationalism between the Young Ireland movement of 1848 and the Fenian Rising of 1867. The evidence to hand would seem to indicate that he tried to steer a middle course between nationalism and acceptance of the *status quo*. A past pupil makes the following comment:

Father Paul always showed strict neutrality in these troubled times, and even in his lectures on Irish history, we could never gather what were his personal opinions as to the merits or demerits of the cause for which so many of his erstwhile pupils were condemned to prison or exile. He would, however, impress on us that it would be all for the better to forget in many respects 'the days of old' and remember the days to come, and the possibilities of what they were likely to hold for us. He believed that Irish boys could hold their own with any others.... His counsels were many, but, like the commandments, could be reduced to two – truth and honesty. (Allen, 147)

Views on education

In addition to possessing an inherent courtesy and graciousness, Paul was also broad-minded and tolerant. Protestant parents had no hesitation in sending their children to the Monastery School which he built in Milltown: there were some half dozen attending the school in 1844, despite the fact that the town contained not only a Protestant (Church of Ireland) School, but also a Presbyterian and a Wesleyan one. Even more notable, however, was Paul's positive attitude towards, and acceptance of, the system of education under the supervision of the National Board. When compared with the relations of the Christian Brothers with this Board, Paul's attitude would seem not only significant but strikingly anomalous.

The Irish National Schools

The Irish National Schools are of considerable significance, not only in the history of education in Ireland, but in also in that of some other English-speaking countries, because they were the first attempt at a non-denominational State system of education in the British Empire. First established in 1831, these schools, though theoretically non-denominational, gradually, over the years, became *de facto* denominational schools.

This latter evolution, however, took many years and, especially in the second and third quarters of the century, there was deep division among the clergy and hierarchy on the question of the National Board. Dr Murray, Archbishop of Dublin, took the view that the system gave sufficient freedom to Catholic teachers to give the essentials of Catholic education. While the majority of the Irish Bishops agreed with him, some sided with Dr John McHale, Archbishop of Tuam, who maintained that the ethos of the National Schools was opposed to that of the ideal Catholic school. Though McHale appealed to Rome on the matter, Propaganda, after some initial dithering, ultimately refused to legislate on the question, leaving it to the local ordinary to decide whether or not to support the National Schools in his own diocese. (Feheney, 12)

The dissatisfaction of the Christian Brothers with the National Schools began in the lifetime of Edmund Rice. That Edmund himself initiated the movement to sever the connection of the Brothers with the National Board, or was even personally anxious to do so, is, as yet, however, far from established beyond doubt. This is not to deny that, at the 1836 General Chapter, a specially-appointed Committee of Five recommended withdrawal from the National Board and had its recommendation accepted. Moreover, the Chapter, in Plenary Session, passed a resolution to the effect that 'a connection with the Board of National Education .. would ultimately prove fatal to the religious as well as to the professed object of the Institute'. (Normoyle, 281)

Edmund Rice, when informing Dr Murray of the decision of the General Chapter of 1836 to withdraw some of the Brothers' schools from the National Board, makes it clear that this was not necessarily his own personal decision: 'I have to inform your Grace that, at our last Chapter, it was decreed...' (Normoyle, 283). Though few would contend that the National Schools were all that Edmund Rice would like his schools to be, a close study of the proceedings of his council and the minutes of the chapters of the time makes it clear that his immediate advisers brought significant pressure to bear on him to sever his connection with the National Board. There was a forceful and articulate anti-National Board lobby among Edmund's confrères in the Christian Brothers, just as there was among the hierarchy.

Paul and the National Board
It is important to remember that the direct connection between the Presentation Brothers and Edmund Rice formally ended in the autumn of 1826 when Brother Riordan left the North Monastery and came to the South Parish, Cork, under the immediate authority of Bishop Murphy. Though trained as one of Edmund Rice's followers, Brother Riordan and his early companions, including Paul, had to make their own decisions, under the general authority of Bishop Murphy, from 1826 onwards. Their attitude towards the National Board of Education was similar to that of Edmund Rice in the early years of that institution. This attitude could be succinctly expressed as one of reluctant co-operation. In 1836, as we saw above, Edmund and his council decided to sever their connection with the National Board and make

all the Christian Brothers schools private. The Presentation Brothers, under Brother Michael Augustine Riordan, on the other hand decided to continue their association with the Board.

One of the most practical effects of severing a connection with the Board was the financial consequences for both teachers and pupils. It meant that the Christian Brothers had to charge the children more for schoolbooks and either the parish or the parents had to contribute to the upkeep of the Brothers. The Presentation Brothers, on the other hand, were paid a capitation grant in lieu of salaries by the National Board and schoolbooks were supplied at cost price to the children. If the Presentation Brothers had any significant complaint against the Board, it was merely the reluctance of the latter in certain instances to grant affiliation to new schools. (Powis, Q.17,303)

Paul and the Powis Committe

In 1868 Paul appeared before the Powis Committee of Inquiry into Primary Education. He professed himself satisfied with the books of the National Board and had no objection to their covert Protestant tone or overt moralising (Powis, Q.17305). After severing their connection with the Board, the Christian Brothers, on the other hand, wrote and published their own set of textbooks but had to charge the children the retail price of these books (Powis, Q. 9317). It will be seen in another contribution in this volume that this charge could sometimes involve considerable hardship for poor people in Cork at that time. Writing about his early schooldays around the time of the Powis Inquiry, Conroy says:

> I was sent first to the Christian Brothers in Blarney Lane...but the lesson books were so expensive that I can yet see the sad face of my mother who could not afford the price of the new books needed whenever I was promoted. (Conroy, p. 41, this volume)

Paul also had no objection, as the Christian Brothers had, in accepting the National Board's directive that religious instruction be confined to a specific time of the day and so listed on the school timetable. He believed in keeping religious instruction separate from secular instruction. He even went so far as to say that he would never mix the two on the grounds that religious instruction was too solemn to have it mixed up with secular instruction (Powis, Q.17293).

In these respects, Paul's evidence differs significantly from that of Brother John Augustine Grace, who was the official representative of the Christian Brothers. Brother Grace found that the rules of the National Board restricted him and his companions 'very much' in so far as they felt that they were 'not permitted to teach in a Catholic spirit' (Powis, Qs.9,294-5). Paul, on the other hand, contended that, not only did he not experience any inconvenience in operating the rules of the National Board, but that, even if the Presentation Schools were separated from the Board, he would not be disposed to make any change in the distribution of time for religious instruction (Powis, Q.17, 283). There was, therefore, at least in 1868, a significant difference between the attitudes of the two congregations owing their origin to Edmund Rice towards co-operation with the Irish National Board of Education.

The stand taken by Paul before the Powis commission, being so much at odds with that of Brother Grace, representing the Christian Brothers, was a cause of tension between the two Congregations (O'Toole). And while Paul's evidence was undoubtedly at variance with the policy of the leadership of the Christian Brothers, especially from 1836 onwards, it is far from clear that it was in opposition to the private sentiments of Edmund Rice himself. At the time of the 1836 General Chapter, Edmund, as Superior General, was under pressure from several directions. His plan to use the profits from pay schools to finance schools for poor children was being attacked by a faction led by his successor, Paul Riordan (not to be confused with Michael Augustine Riordan), who regarded pay schools as anathema. There was also pressure from the same group to reform the structure of the General Council of the Congregation. And, finally, there was the anti-National Board lobby, in which, again, Paul Riordan was prominent. It is a moot point, therefore, whether, even if Edmund Rice felt strongly that the connection with the

National Board should be maintained, he had sufficient physical stamina and self-confidence at that particular stage of his life to win general support for his view.

The late Brother Leonard O'Toole CFC has suggested that Edmund Rice, if allowed room to manoeuvre by the 1836 General Chapter, would not have severed his connection with the National Board (O'Toole). This point is important in any consideration of the contribution of the followers of Edmund Rice to popular education in Ireland. It raises the question as to whether or not the nature of that contribution, subsequent to the death of the Founder, was entirely along the lines envisaged by him.

The evidence of Brother Paul is of some significance in any evaluation of the attitude of the Christian Brothers towards the National Board and their decision to terminate affiliation and set up what was tantamount to an opposition system of primary education in Ireland. The Christian Brothers have explained this decision by claiming that the subsequent history of the Board justified the fears of the anti-national Board lobby within the Congregation. Normoyle, its premier historian, calls the decision 'both historic and heroic' and sees the Congregation renouncing its claim to Government aid in preference to sacrificing its principles (Normoyle, 282-3).

A study of the views of Paul Townsend, however, indicates that there was an alternative approach, even at that time.

Paul Townsend, though not unique, was atypical of Roman Catholic clergy and religious of the second half of the nineteenth century in having a positive attitude towards the National Board of Education. This is not to say that he was not familiar with the system and did not understand it thoroughly, or was unaware of its dangers, but he seemed to believe that, ultimately, how the system was mediated to the pupils depended on the teacher. And his own experience convinced him that the good teacher had enormous influence on his pupils.

It should, however, be pointed out that in his evidence before the Powis Committee of 1868, Brother Paul's fellow Presentation Brother, Alphonsus L. Gaynor, fell somewhat short of Paul in his approval of the Board, though he, also, was unequivocal in stating that he experienced no difficulty with the rules of the Board when imparting religious instruction to the children (Powis, Q.17, 363).

Influence of Paul in educational policy

Brother Paul's attitude of co-operation with the National Board, and his ability to maintain a religious atmosphere in the school, while honouring the regulations of the Board, did not pass unnoticed. A former junior teacher at the Lancasterian School, who emigrated to the USA but retained his interest in education later wrote about it:

> The schools were National ones, although, taught by Brothers, a most equitable arrangement, and, as such, without any expense to the parish or people, and I cannot understand to this day why some priests employ lay teachers in their parishes, or even employ the Christian Brothers, who are admirable teachers, but necessarily an added expense to the poor people especially when the National School System taught by the [Presentation] Brothers is so superior in its methods. (Feheney, 13)

Beloved of his pupils

A past pupil, writing in 1880 on learning of Brother Paul's death in the South Monastery, sums up the feelings of many of his past pupils:

> I cannot tell you what a flood of pleasant memories rushed through my mind on reading of Brother Paul's death. In my wanderings to and fro over this little world of ours, my mind often returns to the scenes and surroundings of my boyhood, and prominent amongst my recollections of such stands Mr Townsend. I can never forget the angelic kindly old man – he was one of the grandest characters it has ever been my lot to come across. His childish simplicity, his humility and deep piety drew children towards him with feelings of confidence; whilst his keen relish of wit and humour, and his sympathetic and cheerful disposition endeared him to his pupils as if he were a fond parent (Allen, 149).

For me, I can never forget the kindly interest he took in my welfare, and there must be a great many, who, like myself, owe – in no remote degree – their success in life to him. One of the dearest wishes of my life is, that my sons will have a preceptor and such an example and incentive to good as I had in Father Paul. (Allen, 148)

Dr Higgins, Bishop of Kerry, and a past pupil of Brother Paul, paid him a very generous tribute of comparing him with the clergy, saying, 'Neither in nor out of Maynooth College did I ever meet his equal'. The writer of the Annals in the Presentation Monastery, Milltown, said of him, 'He was a perfect gentleman. No one could converse with him without realising his nobility of character and feeling oneself in the presence of one whose noble bearing and outstanding virtues commanded respect.' (Allen, 149)

Conclusion

Paul Townsend is a neglected personality in the history of education in Cork and, more regrettably, in the history of his own Congregation, the Presentation Brothers. He is a person, moreover, whose ideas on education are worthy of more research. This might, conceivably, be done within the context of a study of the Lancasterian School, of which he was Superintendent for twenty-three years. He undoubtedly had a vision of education for the poor, in line with, and arguably in harmony with that of his founder, Edmund Rice.

We have called him an exemplar of the tradition of Edmund Rice within the Presentation Brothers. This is not to say that he was trained by Edmund, or even met him more than once, and that only probably, but that in his life and work he continued a tradition begun by Edmund and gave expression to values that were dear to the Founder. These included a great practical love of and devotion to poor children; an idealism and unselfishness that enabled him to commit himself to the realisation of the Kingdom of God on earth and in so doing make use of every talent he possessed. Paul was also gifted with a pleasing personality characterised by graciousness, benevolence and geniality that made him beloved of young and old. Moreover, though modest and humble, he had a self-confidence and independence of mind that enabled him to see the road ahead and follow without fear where his conscience beckoned.

NOTES

1. In keeping with the editorial policy outlined in the Introduction to this volume, referencing will be kept to a minimum. This article is an extended version of the more fully-referenced article, by J. Matthew Feheney, 'Br Paul Townsend, 1798-1881', published in *Presentation Studies*, No. 1 (1982), 10-15. Reference has also been made in the text to the following works:

Allen, D.H., *The Presentation Brothers* (1993, Presentation Brothers, Cork).
Normoyle, MC, *A Tree is Planted* (1975, 2nd ed. 1976, Christian Brothers, Dublin).
O'Toole, Leonard, Lecture on 'Renewal in the Spirit of the Founder' at Presentation College, Reading, Berks, England, 28 October, 1980.
Report of the Royal (Powis) Commission on Primary Education. Minutes of Evidence, B.P.P. XXVIII, Pt III.1 & IV.1. Microfiche 76. Termed Powis Report in text after the chairman, Lord Powis.

TWO TEACHERS

Sean O'Faolain
(From *Vive Moi!*)

Editor's Note: John Whelan, later known as Sean O'Faolain, was born in 3 Mardyke Place, next door to Presentation College, Mardyke, Cork. Later the family moved to a larger house in Half Moon Street. He spent fourteen years in two Presentation Brothers' schools, the first ten at the Lancasterian School (The Lancs), Washington Street, and the last four at Presentation College (Pres). Though he has also written about his time in The Lancs, the limited space available will permit us to reprint here only part of the section in his autobiographical Vive Moi! dealing with his years in Pres. We have retained his own title, 'Two Teachers', for the chapter even though he really speaks about three: Brother E.J. Connolly (The Man), Mr Edward (Doggy) Sheehan and Pádraig Ó Domhnaill.

From my crazy-happy Lancasterian National School I duly followed the trail of my two elder brothers into the secondary or higher school run by the same order, known to the public as the Presentation Brothers' College and to its pupils as the Pres, with the final s pronounced as a z. Fees here were a large worry to my parents, even though the headmaster kindly granted my father special rates. I could list other acts of kindness by him, such as the loan of expensive books like good dictionaries, efforts to throw a few pounds in my way for the private tutoring of backward pupils, and – I now suspect – much patient forbearance with a boy whom he must have considered egregious, or odd, or worse...

The Pres, in my time, which is now a long time ago, was a fake in every respect except two. It provided some sort of pseudo-religious education, and it was a useful cramming factory for the sons of less well-heeled parents – clerks, civil servants, lay teachers and the like. In this latter it sometimes succeeded to remarkable effect when it got hold of specially bright students. It was also the useful gateway through which a small number of youths entered the local college of the National University, there, if they were industrious, to become doctors, engineers, secondary teachers, and the like. The majority went to modest posts in banks, insurance, the railways. If any reader feels that in doing so much the Pres did all it could do, I have to say that there were other schools, managed by priests, at that same time, and subject to similar governmental controls, which adapted themselves with subtlety and sophistication to the task of providing a Christian education with a humanist bias. One such was James Joyce's Jesuit School at Clongowes Wood, and whatever that school may now think of Joyce, he always paid high tribute to his Jesuit teachers. In fairness, however, we must remember that Clongowes Wood not only drew boys from much better-class homes than ours, but was a boarding school where the Jesuits had the boys all day long, for games, debating societies, and cultural doings of every kind. They did no less well at examinations than cramming schools like ours.

The worst about the Pres I must admit at once and be done with it – the place was snobby: it was the very essence of genteelism. It was an imitation of something else somewhere else. But, to be sure, the whole of urban Ireland at that time was an imitation of something else somewhere else; and it was the dilemma of the Pres, and all of urban Ireland, that it had to be so. To be of any use it had to accept the fact of life of the same imperial pattern and hierarchy that my father had accepted, to fit us all into it, to help us all to succeed within it. How few escaped, could escape, or wished to escape that trap! If James Joyce had half an ounce of social conscience, of Stendhal's or Balzac's awareness of the moulding power of the cash-nexus, he would have made this clear in his *Portrait of the Artist as a Young Man*. He made it most near to clear when he contrasted Daedalus the poor rebel – but not against both the Empire and the Church – with Buck Mulligan, who set out to conform. My school produced some rebels but not many; it produced conformists by the ton.

I have no wish to dally over my four years in the Pres I have an idea that I have spent a good part of my life labouring under the same wish. My unhappiness there was chronic and suppressed. Even to this late day my two most frequent nightmares bring me back either there or to the period of the Troubles, each always leaving me with an identical, detestable impression of having been helplessly coerced. Those nightmares were often associated in my earlier manhood with the image of myself as a pea or a little glass marble under the towering overhang of a vast globe, large as the world, about to roll over me. If there is anything at all rebellious, obstinate or even mulish in my nature, and I think there is, it either began to take form at this time of subjection or, if it was latent in me from the moment of my birth, it flourished then like the banyan.

The prison gates closed on me the first day I started to cram French, Latin and algebra at breakback speed, an experience for whose drudgery it is not possible to find adequate language. Again, in fairness, I must say that although punishment was the sole spur within the school, by far the more painful spur came from outside the school: my father's and mother's repeated reminders that all this wonderful education was costing them great hardship and that, for their sake as well as my own, I must profit by it. Since there was no escape from this loving blackmail there were many occasions when I almost hated my parents for enduring so much for love of me.

I recall a typical occasion with a particular shame and bitterness. On this day the whole of my class, on being refused early release from school to go to the Cork Park Races, a great annual event which had always hitherto meant that classes were cut short, rebelled in a body and did not return after the lunch break – all, that is, except three boys, two others and myself. We pleaded, quite honestly, that we did not mind being punished, if punishment ensued, but that we could not bear that our parents should be, as we knew they would be, hurt and shocked. (The parents of the two other fellows were teachers in city schools.) The next day the massed rebels were duly caned, one by one, while we three sat, heads hanging, ashamed and unmanned. Remembering that day, I was to write one of my best stories, 'Up the Bare Stairs', about a man who went through that school and passed out of it to an eminent career inspired wholly by desire to escape from his parents' enslaving love.

I based it also, in part, on a remark of my brother's when in later life I said, to tease him: 'I have been told that there was only one examination in your whole career that you could not pass – a test in the Irish language. It was part of some scholarship exam-ination that would have won you three years free at the university. Is this true?'

'Couldn't pass it?' he laughed. 'I failed it deliberately. I would have had to remain at home for years if I had gone to the uni-versity. My sole ambition was to get out from under at all costs.'

I wished he had not kept that secret to himself: we might have conspired to make home life more easy for both of us.

Only two subjects were presented to me at the Pres with enough feeling to fire my interest: Irish and Latin – the first because I could relate it to life, and the second because the head-master, who was prior of the order, took a few of us brighter boys for Latin in our senior years.

He was the Reverend E. J. Connolly, known to us all as the Man, already old when I sat under him, so old that it was said that he had taught the grandfathers of some of my fellow pupils. He was a slight, smallish man, with a gentle, benevolent, com-manding appearance, his white hair curling out from under his biretta, his voice always soft, his persistent attitude to us boys one of solemn amusement. He seemed to us a saintly man, yet at the same time we recognised in him, with admiration, a force of per-sonality and a shrewd worldliness that none of the other Brothers had. His large family of past students were by my time already scattered all over the world, and he had hung the portraits of about a score of the more distinguished among them in the main corridor for us to admire and emulate: officers in the British Army, colonial judges, men in the Indian Civil, and suchlike. Now and again one of these old boys would drop in to visit him, and he would always bring the visitor to see his old classroom. Once I remember an Australian officer, so tall that, as he looked at the old desks in the old room, and chatted with the Man, he leaned one hand on top of the door. Once a mayor from, I think, Johannesburg came. The Man thus gave us our first glimpse of the world's possibilities. We felt that he held the keys to all sorts of interesting careers in his hands.

He had the name of being a fine Latinist, and when he took us over he conveyed to us, if only by his mere tone of voice and his reverent approach as he recited the verses of Horace, Ovid or Virgil, at least some awareness of the sacred ground we were beginning to explore. I can still hear his caressing voice fondling the familiar phrases:

> *O fons Bandusiae, splendidior vitro,*
> *Dulci digne mero non sine floribus ...*
> (O fountain of Bandusia, shining like crystal, worthy of flowers and a libation of sweet wine ...)

The impression was indelible. Many years after, when following the steps of John Henry Newman in Italy, I visited Castrogiovanni, or Enna, perched high in the centre of Sicily. There I found, at its base, the Lake of Pergusa, where Pluto abducted that fair flower Proserpina while she was gathering flowers far less fair. As I stood by the lake I suddenly heard his old, soft voice murmuring in my ear: *Terra tribus scopulis vastum procurrit in aequor Trinacris* (Sicily pours down to the vast sea its three promontories). And:

> *Tot fuerant illic, quot habet natura, colores:*
> *Pictaque dissimili flore nitebat humus.*
> (There were as many colours there as Nature holds:
> The whole earth painted with motley, gleaming flowers.)

I am sure that under a better system the Man could really have made young Latinists of some of us. He had no time. Too many examinations lay ahead like fences in a four-year race. There was no time to allow us to recite aloud, to talk to us about the authors of those poems or about classical mythology, even to show us a map of the voyages of Aeneas, to show us photographs of Cumae, or Lake Avernus, or the forum Romanum, or Sirmione, to do anything that would relate what we read to life and history. Yet he did give us a sense of form in poetry, he schematised eternal emotions, instilled a sense of immemorial piety, revealed to us that happy marriage of feeling and the intelligence which is the very heart of the classical way of life.

It goes without saying that he had time to do this only in a little way, could open only a postern gate – not even that, a cat's door; that we read no Catullus, or Juvenal, had to wait for our college days to open Pliny or Seneca; that when we read Cicero we had no time to think of Roman politics – in Cicero's day the most exciting politics in the whole history of Rome; that we pursued Caesar and Livy at such a pace that they became dull tasks in mechanical translation that bored us stiff. I suppose even the Commissioners of Education had their excuse for all this savagery. Behind them, no doubt, there lay some other tyranny, including possibly the grim morality of Arnold of Rugby, whom many Latinists blame for cleaning up the classics, as certain other men cleaned up Shakespeare. (Had Sam Johnson gone to Rugby under Arnold, he would not have read his Catullus and Juvenal as avidly as he did at Lichfield.) Apart from what we got from the Man we had time only to cram for examinations to get jobs. That was the sum of it.

An absurd instance of this: one day our English teacher, Doggy Sheehan, said, as was his way: 'Learn off the first sixteen lines of Tennyson's 'Ulysses'.'

The next day the first boy in the class recited rapidly down to *And drunk delight of battle with my peers,* and stopped.

'Go on!' said Doggy.

'That's the sixteen lines, sir.'

'But where did he drink delight of battle?' Doggy implored.

'It's not in the sixteen lines, sir.'

'Not another line?' Doggy sighed. 'Even for the sake of *Far on the ringing plains of windy Troy?* '

But it was not merely Doggy's own mechanical way of saying 'The next sixteen lines for tomorrow' – as if all poetry were in quatrains – that had produced the result he deplored: both he and the boy were identical victims of a universal chain reaction started years ago and elsewhere.

In literary terms Doggy was an aged version of all Chekhov's schoolteachers, that weary, frustrated type we meet as younger men in *The Cherry Orchard* and *The Seagull,* become at last contented, no longer troubled even by remnant dreams. He was tall, thin, shambling, spectacled, bowler-hatted. His little briefcase bore his derisive nickname Doggy scratched by some boy on a patch of leather that had obviously been sewn there to hide the word Doggy scratched beneath it by some earlier tormentor. He had a flat Cork accent, saying 'flaat' for 'flat', or 'waey' for 'way', and all his th's, as in 'this' or 'that', had been, after the common Cork manner, dentalised into d's – 'dis' and 'dat'. He taught, that is he crammed, English poetry, drama and prose, English history, European history, Irish history, and world geography. His methods of cramming so much so quickly may be summed up by observing that the effective text for English history was somebody's outline handled by such injunctions from Doggy as: 'For tomorrow look up the reign of Queen Anne and pick out the dates.' Inevitably, he was a butt – nobody could hold the interest of a class of lively boys under such circumstances. He would be asked 'double-meaning' questions, whose tenor he either ignored or reproved by a sniggering, 'Stop dat now!' His piles of books were slyly toppled from his table. He suffered constant inattention and occasional rowdiness. If it were not that in this senior classroom there usually were at least two other classes, and teachers, and, frequently, the Man himself in a corner coaching two or three boys preparing for special examinations, he would have been quite badgered by us. Yet, as his nickname may suggest, we all liked Doggy. He was harmless, he was necessary, and even we could see that he was put upon.

I more than liked him because he conferred a supreme gift on me. I had his open invitation to drop down, any night I liked, to his old dusty, murky house in the Lower Road, above the Railway Terminus, and there rummage among his books – mottled, dusty, foxed, unread, piled on shelves, chairs, the floor, up the stairs, in the hall, in boxes, on tables, under tables. (He must have spotted a potential book-lover in me: for which I revere him.) He lived in this old house alone with his mother, who was said to have been a midwife, a fat, heavy-breasted, warm old soul who gave to this drape of clothes on two sticks who was our Doggy and her beloved son the surprising personal reality of a name. She spoke of him as Jack. I would pick out a book, attracted by its binding, or its gilt lettering, or the decoration on the spine, and find I held

Congreve's Plays. He would say, 'Dey're Congreve's plays. Some of 'em are dirty. Read 'em.'

I would find a sixpenny paper novel in my dusty hand.

'What's dat you have? Marie Corelli? Very romantic. Don't let your mudder see you readin' it.'

I have wondered whether the books he pressed on me were of his own taste or the midwife's: Hall Caine's *The Manxman,* George Moore's early novels ('Dat fellow was an awful black-guard!'), *Captain Kettle,* Hewlett's *The Forest Lovers,* William de Morgan's *Alice-for-Short,* Countess von Arnim's *Elizabeth* books, Rider Haggard's *She,* Barrie's *Little Minister,* E. F. Benson's *Dodo,* mixed up with practically all of Shaw, Norman Angell's *The Great Illusion,* somebody's *Our German Cousins,* many books about Napoleon. (He had once visited France, and walked all over the site of the Battle of Waterloo.) He ignored the classics. ('I have dem all. But I'm all for the moderns now.') The reader will have noted that most of the books I mention were of the 1890s.

Did his preferences reflect early aspirations – sentimental, military, political? If so, he reached the apex of his ambition when he founded and became first, and last, president of the Cork Consumers' League, a body composed almost entirely of land-ladies, interested chiefly in the prices of domestic supplies.

Chekhov, clearly, exaggerated the sadness of the teacher type. Doggy was a drudge, but not a sad drudge. It is one definition of insanity to have an itch, and of sanity to have a niche. He had made his own modest image of himself. He had found a niche in the city's body politic to enshrine it. So much of life is a pure act of the imagination!

There were other talents whose waste impressed me, but I was most deeply marked by our one rebel, apart from the Man the only teacher there whom I fully admired. He was our Irish language teacher, who let fall, in odd words and phrases, hints about a far-off free country called the West where people talked only in Irish, wove and spun in it, fished and ploughed, drank and laughed in it, where – to me, at any rate, he gave this feeling – there was a wonderland where the star of Eden never died. I was also impressed by another teacher, Christy Flynn, to whom I had no opportunity to come closer than respect. He would pause in a French lesson at, say, the word *bois* to recall with a few fond words Le Bois de Boulogne, or at the word *invalides* to wave a hand across Ireland towards the Seine and Les Invalides. That was true education. In another not wholly dissimilar way the Man would leave a mark when, at five minutes to twelve, he would take out his silver watch, rub its glass between his thumb and his palm, halt lessons with a word he was always uttering, *'Gentlemen!'*, and talk for four minutes about somebody like Marshal Foch ('A daily communicant, gentlemen'), or of his regiment of cuirassiers drawn up before a priest for general absolution before entering battle. (This, of course, was right up my alley, plumes, swords, helmets and all that splendid fudge.) Then, while we were still seeing his picture, he would take off his biretta and lead us into the Angelus at the stroke of noon that, by then, sounded like a bugle calling us to charge!

I must say more about our Irish teacher, Pádraig Ó Domhnaill: young, handsome, eager and quite uncowed. He, too, had his own self-image, as we all discovered the day the news ran through the school that he had been seen in the streets dressed in the full dark-green uniform of the Irish Volunteers (forerunners of the IRA) leading a band of what, I fear, The Man would have called *canaille*, on some military exercise. Had he been any other man I would have scoffed at him. I was on the Man's side, the saintly-worldly side, with Foch and his cuirassiers, with the Indian Civil, Sandhurst, gallant little Belgium, brave little Montenegro, and so on, beside all of which these Irish Volunteers were nothing but vulgar corner-boys' nonsense. But I so admired Ó Domhnaill as a man that this wind of rumour about him ran over me with the shiver of a question and a doubt. Besides, I gathered that he had worn a handsome uniform with a hat pinned up on one side. 'Was there a plume on it?' I asked eagerly, and felt disappointed when they said, 'No, no plume.' I have talked earlier of pools brimming and fountaining. The brimmings one can more or less easily recall and record; not so easily the last glorious moments of pouring-over, of fountaining revelation, chiefly because they so often come not with a sense of triumph but of surrender. So it was with me and the revelation of the Rising of 1916 for which young Ó Domhnaill was preparing.

My heart did not burst with excitement and joy when I heard that a rising had broken out in Dublin that Easter Monday morning of 1916. I had not more than a week previous seen somebody, who might have been Pádraig Ó Domhnaill, drilling a shamble of forty or fifty men in the open place beneath our windows in Half Moon Street – rudely accoutred fellows, with no uniform other than a belt around their ordinary working clothes, only a very few bearing rifles. As I watched them fumble and stumble my blood had curled against them, they were so shabby, so absurd, so awkward, so unheroic-looking. They were, as my father said, as the Man would have said, disgracing our country: and this while real, glorious war was flashing and booming in Flanders and France. When we heard of the Rising my father and I raged at its betrayal. The British Army would clean 'those fellows' up in twenty-four hours. Then they would all get what they damn well deserved – the low ruffians, the common corner-boys! Only bit by bit did my loyalties veer as the days passed, one by one, and I found that they were still holding out. Dublin was shelled and burning, that noble city I had traversed with poor Tom Boyhan, now dead in France, but still they were holding out. There was a charge by British cavalry down O'Connell Street, in the best G. A. Henty, Light Brigade tradition of gallant lunacy, and I, who should have been all for that splendid gesture, felt the world turning around in my stomach when I heard, with satisfaction, that the ruffians and corner-boys had mowed them down. I continued to resist until the final surrender, and that broke me. Irishmen were surrendering to Englishmen, with dignity. That day I stole away up to my attic, and knelt on the scrubbed floor and looked out over the roofs of Cork under its tent of clouds, and I wept for them. When, in the following weeks, the British took out the leaders and shot them in ones, and twos, and threes, everybody and everything I had believed in began to tumble about me. Henty, my father, my home. The Man held out longest, because although he disapproved of the whole thing he was mild in his reproof. 'Foolishness!' he said. 'Foolishness on all sides!' For another long time, two years and more, I held out with him.

I noticed one day that Ó Domhnaill, who was still with us

after 1916, was wearing a plain gold ring in his lapel and asked him what it meant. He explained that what he was wearing was *An Fáinne*, the Irish words for 'The Ring', a token which meant that whoever wore it could converse in our native tongue with anybody he met who also wore it. I at once told him I wanted to belong to this circle, and he encouraged me to prepare for the oral test. He began to talk to me in Irish whenever he had the chance. He told me I should start reading poetry and prose aloud, and loaned me a couple of books of Irish verse for the purpose.

One of these books contained the simple Gaelic verses of one Tomás Ó Súilleabháin, a Kerry postman of the nineteenth century. I kept the book for years. I cherished it solely for its frontispiece – a smudgy photograph showing a rocky promontory on the Atlantic, a ruined chapel, an old graveyard, a few small fields. Time out of mind I used to open the book at this photograph and gaze and gaze at it. Sea, chapel, graveyard, lonely rock, poor fields - they became my new symbols, transfigured by my longing for that liberty from my passionate flesh in a romantic, nobly patterned world which I now equated with remoteness, hardness, age and a traditional life whose pieties they rounded. It was not the place in the photograph that I revered or wished to possess but the absoluteness or essence of the entire life that I imagined made it, so that what I was really shaping in my mind whenever I looked at that photograph was a myth of life for which, so far, the only bodily vessel I knew was the wet, worn plain of West Limerick, with its lichened limestone walls, its distant sea, its battered Norman ruins, its dead, my dead. Gazing at that picture, I was creating a new legend, a new myth. I was unconsciously writing it, peopling it. I was engaged in every writer's first task – hypothesising life, imagining himself in it, as it, another Adam, self-created, fecund.

My new symbols were, of course – I say 'of course' because such is the course of nature – exhaustible symbols. Most symbols are. That apple, also, would fall with a whisper from its tree. Yet, before it fell life was to seem one long summer, many years of it, during which I was to know the reality behind those appealing images and during which the tree that bore them had to die for everybody else as well as me. All art, Pater said, is life seen through a temperament. One modifies one's views but one's temperament is a given thing, an indestructible and unalterable necessity.

Thanks to Ó Domhnaill, I was wearing my Fáinne in the summer of 1917. That summer I went for the last time to County Limerick with my mother. I remember very little of that holiday. I remember my Uncle John, on the farm, laughing and saying, 'Haha, John, I see they're making a fine, tall, straight young man out of you!' I remember cycling about the country on my own in search of old abbeys and castles, such as the ruined castle of the last of the Desmond earls at Askeaton, or the friary of the Kildare earls at Adare. In a dim, general way I recall wandering around the Commons when my uncle would be at work on his humble plots of ground, or sitting daydreaming for hours by the lake, or walking the small white limestone roads – once with a purpose: to see Curragh Chase, where the poet Aubrey de Vere lived – or merely lying in the high-walled cottage orchard on Roche's Road reading, reading, reading, or idly watching the swifts dart like bullets into the ivy hanging a foot thick on the walls, or the Atlantic clouds passing ever so slowly from wall to wall, and not a sound but the inevitable crowing cock far away, or the dim clop of a straying horse's hooves.

The school year after that summer was my last, and it was climactic.

I was now eighteen, and by this time we were all for the Rebels, but still only as an idea, unembodied. The Pres, and the Man, so far changed as to allow a group of us to start a hurling team – hitherto the only game played in the school had been 'English' rugby. The Man gazed at me in amused surprise the first day he saw me going off with my hurley stick of new white ash and my togs. 'You?' he said. 'Games?' For my part, it was merely an effort to give body to my vague rebelly ideas, and it took some doing, because although Uncle John might say I was fine and straight I was also skinny, had never played any games, and was deeply conscious of how silly I looked with my long spindly legs in white shorts, running helplessly and uselessly around the field after the flying ball, so inept that my fellows had to beg me to desist because I was a danger to them (and to myself) with my wild swinging ash. That summer I won, with difficulty, an entrance scholarship to the university, and that summer the Man so far yielded to the new winds blowing over Ireland as to permit the college to be used as a summer school open to the public at large, men and women, young and old, for the teaching of Irish. Again encouraged by Ó Domhnaill, I attended it. Here, having done his work, he drops out of my story. No other man has influenced my life so much and so quietly as he.

THE MADWOMAN OF CORK
Patrick Galvin

Today
Is the feast day of Saint Anne
Pray for me
I am the madwoman of Cork.

Yesterday
In Castle Street
I saw two goblins at my feet
I saw a horse without a head
Carrying the dead
To the graveyard
Near Turner's Cross.

I am the madwoman of Cork
No one talks to me.

When I walk in the rain
The children throw stones at me
And women close their doors.
When I die
Believe me
They'll set me on fire.

I am the madwoman of Cork
I have no sense.

Sometimes,
With an eagle in my brain
I can see a train
Crashing at the station.
If I told people that
They'd choke me –
Then where would I be ?

I am the madwoman of Cork
The people hate me.

When Canon Murphy died
I wept on his grave
That was twenty-five years ago.
When I saw him just now
In Dunbar Street
He had clay in his teeth
He blessed me.

I am the madwoman of Cork
The clergy pity me.

I see death
In the branches of a tree
Birth in the feathers of a bird.
To see a child with one eye
Or a woman buried in ice
Is the worst thing
And cannot be imagined.

I am the madwoman of Cork
My mind fills me.

I should like to be young
To dress up in silk
And have nine children.
I'd like to have red lips
But I'm eighty years old
I have nothing
But a small house with no windows.

I am the madwoman of Cork
Go away from me.

And if I die now
Don't touch me.

I want to sail in a long boat
From here to Roche's Point
And there I will anoint the sea
With oil of alabaster.

I am the madwoman of Cork
And today is the feastday of
Saint Anne.
Feed me.

FAOI ANÁIL ÉAMOIN BHEANNAITHE RÍS

Liam Mac Mathúna

Lá aoibhinn samhraidh agus mo mháthair is an chuid eile againn den líontí ag sábháilt an fhéir i 'nDáil Éireann', bhuail comharsa bhéal dorais isteach sa mhóinéar chugainn in éineacht le fear breá lúfar a bhí gléasta in éadaí dubha agus bóna cruaidh bán. Chuir an chomharsa an stróinséir in aithne dúinn agus tugadh mise ina láthair. An Bráthair Aquinas Neville (de Niadh) a bhí ann agus shocraigh sé le mo mháthair go mbuailfimis beirt leis in óstán i nDrom Collachair a bhí dhá mhíle slí uainn, lá áirthe an tseachtain dár gcionn. Bhí m'athair ar Shlí na Fírinne le ceithre bliana faoin am seo. An bhliain 1926 a bhí ann, bliain an dóiteáin scannraithigh a sciob naonúr is daichead chun a mbáis ar ócáid léirithe an scannáin 'Deich nAitheanta Dé' i sean-lochta i lár an bhaile. Go raibh Flaitheas Dé mar leaba acu uile, m'athair féin ina measc!

Le linn an chruinnithe leis an mBráthair Aquinas chuir sé roinnt ceisteanna orm agus bhí orm giota as *Timire an Chroí Ró-Naofa* do léamh. Bhí sé sásta de réir dealraimh agus shocraigh sé go rachainn go hArd Naomh Iosaef um Mheán Fomhair na bliana sin, in éineacht le Séamus ÓSúilleabháin as Drom Collachair a bhí cheana féin mar mhac léinn sa mhainistir.

Tháinig an lá imeachta nuair d'fhág mé slán ag gach éinne sa bhaile, an madra dubh is bán, Seip, chomh maith. Nách mbeinn thar n-ais um Nollaig! Ach mo léan géar! Rinneadh athrú ar na Rialacha agus bhí orm fanacht go h-am samhraidh na bliana dar gcionn, rud nár thaitnigh linne ná lenár muintir sa bhaile. Bhí an chéad cheacht ar féindiúltú foghlamtha agam.

An Bráthair Aquinas a bhí inár gceannas i Roinn na Sóisear. Fear stuama fíor-chineálta deabhóideach ab ea é agus an-tuiscint aige do dhaoine óga. Is cuimhin liom a rá leis uair amháin go dtugadh mo mháthair 'crúiscín salts' dom anois is arís. Chonaic mé an meangadh gáire ar a aghaidh. 'Krushen salts', ar seisean. Thug sé dom mo 'chrúiscín salts'.

Tar éis tamaill h-aistríodh é go post cabhrach do mháistir na nóibhíseach, An Bráthair Breandán Ó Cearrúill, agus tugadh cúram na sóisear don Bhráthair Pius ÓBriain, (a fuair bás mar shagart i Sasana anonn 'sna blianta) agus an Bráthair Finín Ó Ginidhe mar chúntóir aige. Chuireadar beirt Cumann Gaelach ar bun agus toghadh mé féin mar fhear cinn agus mar aitheantas ar an bpost sin cuireadh im shuí ag ceann an bhoird sa bhialann mé in a n-aice féin. Bhíodar araon go han-díograiseach i dtaobh na Gaeilge agus an léinn i gcoitinne agus bhíomar uile an-cheanúil orthu. Níorbh fhada gur ghlac an Bráthair Pius a mhóideanna solúnta deireannacha agus nuair a chonaic mé sínte ar úrlár an tséipéil é ina aibíd bhán searmanais ba bheag nár tháinig na deora óm shúile. Ní fios dom cén fáth.

Cuireadh scrúdú béil orainn sa Ghaeilge roimh dhul abhaile dúinn ar laethanta saoire na bliana 1927, agus bhuaigh Seoirse Turnbul an duais a bhronn an Bráthair Breandán air, *Eochair-Sciath an Aifrinn* – leabhar paidreacha i nGaeilge. Ba mhór mar chuaigh i bhfeidhm orm paidreacha na maidine a bhíodh á rá againn roimh an gcéad rang staidéir.

Ar fhilleadh dúinn tar éis Mí an Mheithimh ar saoire sa bhaile cuireadh ar tástáil sinn mar nuasacháin ar feadh sé mhí sul ar glacadh mar nóibhísigh sinn. Duine diaganta díongbháilte dob ea an Bráthair Breandán Ó Cearrúil, Máistir na Nóibhíseach, ach, tar éis bliana nó mar sin, toghadh in a Uachtarán é agus tháinig an Bráthair De Sales Mehigan anall ó Shasana chun dul i gceannas ar an Nóibhíseacht. Níor thuigeamar an t-am sin gur duine den chéad dream de iondúirí an Oird é ag dul siar chomh fada le 1879. Fear an-léanta, an-phraicticiúil, an-chráifeach úiríseal ann féin é agus é an-tugtha do dhul chun cinn na Nóibhíseach i gcúrsaí oideachais chomh maith le cúrsaí diagachta. Cé nach raibh an Ghaeilge aige féin chuireadh sé mar léitheoireacht spioradálta dúinn *Beathaisnéis ár dTiarna* i nGaeilge leis an Ollamh, An Dr Ó Rathaille, Uachtarán Choláiste na hOllscoile i gCorcaigh. Scríobh sé leabhar do dhaoine faoi chúrsa spioradálta is a chleachtadh, leabhar eolais ar chúrsaí sláinte, agus rinne sé eagarthóireacht ar fhoilseachán dá chuid féin – *Catholic Life.*

Ag cabhrú linn inár gcúrsa léinn thagadh an Bráthair Breandán (Uachtarán) isteach go rialta ag cur lenár n-eolas ar Laidin tríd an soiscéal a léamh i Laidin. Bhí leabhairín dubh a raibh na ceithre soiscéalta ann ag gach duine againn.

An Bráthair Augustine Ó Catháin a mhúineadh matamaitic dúinn. Bhí sé an-tugtha do chuideoga a réiteach agus úsáid na snaoise. Agus maidir le loghanna agus mion-phaidreacha ag dul leo ní raibh aon teorainn lena chuid eolais orthu. Ba bheag nár chuaigh sé i bhfeidhm orainn gurab ionann pinse snaoise a ghlacadh agus anam a scaoileadh as an bPurgadóir. Fear fíor-lách dob ea é. Bhí pictiúr de féin imeasc roinnt óganach ón mainistir in Árd Naomh Iosaef ar crochadh in aice leis an séipéal agus scríofa faoi bhí 'They who instruct many unto justice shall shine as stars for all eternity'.

Níl amhras orm ná go bhfuil sé féin ina réalt gléineach sa bhfiormaimint neamhdha anois. Conas d'fhéadfadh Dia na Glóire cluas bhodhar a thabhairt do na mílte anam gléigeal a cuireadh ar eitilt neamhdha tríd an iliomad loghanna a thuill an Bráthair Caoin Augustine ar a son?

Furaireamar treoir is oiliúint in ár dTeanga Dhúchais ón Iar-Ard Uachtarán, An Bráthair Tomás Ó 'Rathaille (An Bráthair Aloysius). Fear ard téagartha dea-chumtha lúfar dob ea é, ach croí linbh ina chorp oll-mhór. Thabharfadh sé focail an bhailéid ag cur sios ar laoch 1798, Bagnal Harvey chun cuimhne: 'Seven feet was his height with some inches to spare and he looked like a king in command'.

Bhí sé ciúin-bhriathrach cneasta agus saoithiulacht á scaoileadh uaidh i ngné is i gcruth. File, scoláire, ceoltóir, saoi agus duine cráifeach úiríseal b'ea é. Chuir sé dhá leabhar dánta ar fáil – An Spideoigín – Aesop's Fables aistrithe go Gaeilge i bhfoirm filíochta agus ceol a chum sé féin ag gabháil leo; agus An Cuaichín Draíochta, gur glacadh leis ag An Roinn Oideachais mar théacsleabhar don Mheán-Teistméireacht. Agus é imithe go mór in aois thuill sé an gradam M.A. tríd an Odyssey a aistriú go Gaeilge.

B'é an Bráthair Aloysius an dara Árd-Uachtarán ar an Institiúd. Toghadh é sa bhliain 1905 tar éis báis don chéad Ard-Uachtaráin, An Bráthair Pádraig Seighin. Thoghadh arís don dara tréimhse é deich mbliana é go dtí 1925, ní nach ionadh. An Bráthair Aonghas Peadar MacCurtáin a bhí ina chomharba air ó 1925-1937.

Bhíomar dall an uair úd ar an bhfogasgaol crábhaidh a bhí
againn le céad chomhaltaí na hInstitiúide. Fiú amháin b'é Riail
Ban Rialta na Toirbhearta sa mhéad, le h-athruithe oiriúnacha
d'fhir, a bhí fós i bhfeidhm suas go 1925 nuair a chuir an Pápa a
Bheannacht ar Riail Nua a glacadh ag Caibidil na mBráithre
roimhe sin. Chonaic mé féin cóipeanna de Riail Nano Nagle sa
mhainistir agus mé im Nóibhíseach.

Fear mór gnímh chun oideachais dob ea an Bráthair Peadar
agus lean an Bráthair Angelus Ó Catháin a lorg siúd nuair a
tháinig sé i gcumhacht sa bhliain 1937. Bhí sé tar éis seal a
chaitheamh i gCeanada. Is lena linn mar Ard-Uachtarán a
cuireadh tús le misinéireacht sna hIndiacha Thiar (Trinidad) ar
iarratas an Ard-Easpaig Ó Riain, OP. Moladh le Dia uile-
chumhachtach go ndeachaigh obair na misiún úd i dtreise ó shin
agus moladh nach beag dóibh siúd a raibh an misneach acu a
dtoil a chur le Toil Dé chun Fómhair an Tiarna a shábháil. Ár
mbuíochas dóibh seo leanas a rinne an bealach a mharcáil
(1946-49); An Bráthair Canice Ó Coileáin (RIP), An Bráthair
Macartan Ó Síthigh (RIP), An Bráthair Laurence Mac Raghnaill
(Coláiste Mhuire, St Lucia, 1947); An Bráthair Gregory Ó
Síocháin (RIP), An Bráthair Liam Ó Droma (RIP), An Bráthair
Leonard Dennehy (RIP), (St George's College, Grenada, 1947).
Ina measc siúd bhí An Bráthair Dunstan Mac Curtáin,
Uachtarán Réigiúnda, An Bráthair Livinus Ó Ceallaigh (Coláiste
na Toirbhearta, Fernando, Trinidad, 1948). An Bráthair
Bartholomew de Brún, An Bráthair Albert de Faoite (1949). Níos
déanaí cuireadh tús le misiúin i Lima, i bPeru, agus i nGhana san
Aifric.

Is maith is eol do Ard-Uachtarán na linne seo (1996), An
Bráthair StíofánO'Gormáin, na deacrachtaí uafásacha atá ag gabháil leis na misiúin thar sáile mar chaith sé uaidh a phribhléid mar
Phróibhinseach na tíre seo chun dul i mbun gnó imeasc na mbocht
i bPeru. Tá géar-ghá le paidreacha agus cabhair airgid nuair is féidir
le dul chun cínn na dea-oibre a chinntiú. 'Impígí ar Thiarna an
Fhomhair lucht saothraithe a chur chun an fhíonghoirt.'

Cad faoin Dr Ó Conghaile a bhí ina Uachtarán ar Choláiste
na Toirbhearta i gCorcaigh ón mbliain 1892 go dti 1931? 'The
Man' a thugadh ag na scoláirí a bhí faoina chúram air go ceanúil

ómósach, toisc na dea-chomhairle a bhi i dtólamh le fáil uaidh. Ba mhór ar fad ócáid bhronnta Chéim Ónórach L.L.D. ag Ollscoil Chorcaí air ar éirí as an Ard-Mháistreacht dó. B'fhiú an cúntas breá faoin ócáid a léamh i bpáipéir na cathrach. Mar sin fein níor chuir a cháil dá threoir i gcúrsaí cráifeachta é. B'fhacthas é gach oíche ag déanamh Turas na Croise sa séipéal roimh dhul a chodladh dó. B'amhlaidh mar an gcéanna dar ndóigh leis na Bráithre tuata Leo Ó Súilleabháin, Finbarr Ó Brosnacháin, Cuthbert Mac Suibhne, Felix Feaheney, Martin Aherne agus Isidore. Óbhar eiseamláire dúinn iad go léir.

Cainteoir dúchais ó Rinn ó gCuanach dob ea an Bráthair Deaglán O'Súilleabháin, cúntóir sa Nóibhíseacht. D'fhulaing sé go foighneach a pháis féin ag bun na Croise Móire san Óiléar. Is ar éigean a bhí sé riamh gan phian ina cheann agus bhí na néaróga ag cur as dó go mór. Ba nós leis seasamh ag bun na Croise le h-ais cosa tárnálta íomhá Ár dTiarna. Bhí sé go gnaíúil caintech linn i gcónaí.

An Bráthair Fionnbarra Ó Brosnacháin a bhí i gceannas ar an úllord agus nuair a thagadh Mí na Samhna lorgaíodh sé cabhair na nóibhíseach chun an raidhse úll a bhaint is a bhailiú isteach ar nós na mbeach ag cruinniú meala. Le linn na h-oibre sin ar fad bhíodh paidrín an bhráthar ar bogadh trína mhéaranna aige agus é ag rá an Chaplet of Mercy ar son anamacha na marbh i bPurgadóir. Mhúin sé dúinn conas Mionphaidrín na Trócaire a rá agus mhol dúinn é a úsáid mar chabhair do sna h-anamacha ar Leic na Péine. Tamall sul a bhfuair sé bás i seomra na n-easlán dúirt an Bráthair Labhrás Mac Curtáin a bhí ag faire leapa air gur chuala sé é ag labhairt le duine éigin agus gurbh é a thuairim gurbh í an Mhaighdean Mhuire féin a bhí ag comhrá leis.

Deirtear freisin gur chuala an Bráthair Gabriel guthanna Ainglí ag canadh sa séipéal in Ard na Croíche. Níl amhras ar bith ach go bhfuil athrú mór tagtha ar an saol in Éirinn le breis is fiche bliain. Tá laghdú mór ar mhóráltacht go coiteann, cúl á thabhairt leis an Aifreann agus gnásanna spioradálta, agus cúl le cine á thabhairt ag Éireannaigh óga an lae inniu – iad ar sodar i ndiaidh an Ghalldachais atá easpach agus gan treoir. Ach fad is atá spiorad an Rísigh is a chompánaigh, go h-áirithe an Bráthar Micheál Augustine Ó'Riordáin a thug leis inspioráid is spiorad na cráifeachta a bhí léirithe ag an Urramach Iognáid Rís ar bhunú Institiúd na Toirbhearta dó, níl dabht ach go dtabharfar ar bhóthar a leasa na daoine óga atá is a bheidh faoi chúram na mBráithre. Ná dearmhadtar ár Máthair Shíor-Chabrach:

A Mhuire na ngrás a Mháthair Mhic Dé

Go gcuire tú ar mo leas mé....

Ar léamh Imleabhar I de *The Life and Spirituality of Edmund Rice* leis an mBráthair A. O'Toole CFC, dom cuireadh go soiléir ar an eolas mé mar a tugadh an saol cráifeach a chaith an Ríseach (E.R.) ar aghaidh i saol Bhráithre na Toirbhirte í rith na mblianta ó shin i leith. Mar ábhar léitheoireachta againn bhíodh 'The Imitation of Christ', na Soiscéil, agus an saol cráifeach de réir Rodriguez díreach mar a bhíodh leagtha síos ag Iognáid féin i dtosach Ré Réabhlóidigh an Oird.

Bheadh sé do-mhaite dom gan tagairt do fhís chreidiúnach a cuireadh i bhfeidhm in Ard Naomh Iosaef bliain comórtha céad tógáil na mainistreach nuair a cinneadh, ar iarratas Éamoin Rís féin, an teach ollmhór do roinnt le bochtáin na cathrach. An Bráthair Jerome Ó Ceallaigh a bhí ina Árd-Uachtarán ag an am agus b'é a smaoineamh siúd agus cinneadh na Caibidle lena linn a ghlac leis an socrú. An compántas SHARE a rinne an t-athrú agus b'é an Bráthair Jerome a bhí taobh thiar de SHARE an chéad lá riamh agus é mar Uachtarán i gColáiste na Toirbhearta i gCorcaigh. Níl aon teorainn leis an dea-obair ar son na mbocht atá curtha i ngníomh ag an gcomhlacht céanna. An ionadh ar bith é gur chinn Bardas Chorcaí an gradam 'Saoránach Chathair Chorcaí' a bhronnadh ar an mBráthair Jerome i 1994.

Tá sé suimiúil go raibh aithne agam ar an seisear seo leanas as an ochtar déag is fichead de na Bráithre a bhí sa Mhainistir Theas sa bhliain 1878: An Bráthair Felix Feeney, De Sales Mehigan, Leo O'Sullivan, Ignatius Connolly, Peter Curtin, Dominic Walsh, Stanislaus Kenneally. De réir tuairisce sa leabhar leis an mBráthair D. H. Allen FPM, *The Presentation Brothers,* d'eiríodh na Bráithre ag a cúig a chlog gach maidin ó cheann ceann na bliana. Chaitheadh siad suas le dhá uair a chloig ag machnamh ar théama cráifeach ag rá paidreacha agus ag léamh an phortúis' (nó tráthanna Mhuire na maidine mar a cleachtaítí de réir na Rialacha a bhí i bhfeidhm go dtí an t-athrú a deineadh sa bhliain

1989). 'Tar éis Aifrinn ar a seacht bhíodh bricfeasta de arán, tae agus leite acu roimh scaradh chun freastal ar na scoileanna'. Bhíodh dinnéar den ghannchuid acu ar a leath h-uair tar éis a trí tráthnoná. Bhí taithí ar an saol cruaidh gannchúiseach úd ag an mBráthair Albertus Reen a fuair bás cúpla bhliain ó shin in aois an chéid.

Dlúth-chara speisialta liom dob ea an Bráthair Cormac Ó Cearrúil a d'éalaigh uainn go dtí na Flaithis i Samhain na bliana 1992.

Sa bhliain 1974 ag am na Caibidle Próibinsí do phléigh an Bráthair Raymond, Próibhinseach, agus roinnt eile Bráithre le Jerry Sullivan ceist teacht le chéile uair sa bhliain do Bhráithre agus iar-Bhráithre na hInstitiúde. Tar éis díospóireachta glacadh leis go raibh snaidhm cairdis eatarthu agus bunaíodh dá réir Cumann na Toirbhearta (Presentation Association). Thárla an chéad athchaidreamh le chéile ar an 23ú Meithimh 1973 in Óstán an Metropole i gCorcaigh. I láthair bhí na daoine seo leanas: An Bráthair Oirmh Raymond (Próibinseach), Diarmuid Ó Súilleabháin, Seán Breathnach, Seán ÓMurchú, Gearóid ÓHicí, Liam Mac Mathúna, Aodh MacGrianna, Tadhg Ó Murchú, Tadhg Ó Conchúir, Óistín MacCarthaigh, Seanán Ó Murchú, Máirtín Ó Conchúir, Micheál Ó Ceallaigh, Leon Ó Maoldomhnaigh, Diarmuid Céitinn, Seosamh Ó Gadhra, Risteárd Ó Maolagain, Seán Ó Faoláin, Liam Ó Dónaill, Seán Ó Ginidhe, agus Séamus Brennóg.

Chuaigh an Cumann chun cinn ó bhliain go bliain agus tá beartaithe acu Aifreann speisialta céiliúrtha i nGaeilge a chur ar siúl in Árd Naomh Iosaef ag cruinniú na bliana seo (1996) in onóir Éamon Iognáid Rís.

Ba liosta le h-áireamh an oiread sin Bráithre gur bhuail mé leo agus lenar oibrigh mé agus gur mhór é mo ghean orthu. Dúirt na Págánaigh fadó i'dtaobh na gCríostaithe, 'See how these Christians love one another'. Tig liomsa an rud céanna do rá faoi Bhráithre na Toirbhearta a lean agus a leanann fós teagasc agus saoithiúlacht a mbunaitheora spioradálta an Bráthair Urramach Iognáid Rís, atá le bheith ardaithe go foirmeálta imeasc na mBeannaithe ar an cúigiú lá Deireadh Fómhair i mbliana, 1996. Bráithre Críostaí na Toirbhearta!!

In ainneoin an méid Bráithre Críostaí a raibh aithne agam orthu bhraith mé cáirdiúlacht agus taithneamhacht uathu, ag léiriú an ceangal spioradálta idir an dá Institiúd bunaithe ar an mbun-phréamh chéanna.

An teagasc, an oiliúint, an dea-shampla, an chomhairle is an dearcadh spioradálta a fuaireas le linn mo thréimhse imeasc na mBráithre, níl insint ar conas mar a chuaigh siad uile i bhfeidhm orm t.m shaol go n-uige seo. Go n-áirítear clann uile na Toirbhearta imeasc chomhluadair na Bheannaithe, Éamon Iognáid Rís, ar feadh na síoraíochta.

COLLEGE ON A TRAFFIC ISLAND!

Dan Donovan

Time plays funny tricks on us. Recently, while adjudicating a
drama festival in the UCC Granary Theatre on the Mardyke,
Cork, I found myself once again in a familiar and well-loved
place: my old school – Presentation College, where, as a student,
I learned, and, as a teacher, taught, over a period of nearly sixty
years. I first entered what was to become my second home
through the old Western Road gate, before the Mardyke section
had been opened up and developed, in the autumn of 1932.

As I stood in the familiar concrete yard, I began to hear again
the saws cutting down the trees of the old orchard garden
attached to No. 21 Dyke Parade and the mixers preparing concrete for the new extended playground that would link the
Western Road with the Mardyke. In my mind's eye, I could see
again the old sheds running behind the original school buildings
and the coke yard with its great mounds of fuel. This was labou-
riously transported in a wheelbarrow by Denis Buckley, or Bill
Hannon, to the old furnace under the lunch room, until oil-fir-
ing mercifully reduced the drudgery. It was a quiet afternoon and
I reflected on the extraordinary contrast in the noise levels of a
school, from the screaming, shouting and play of hundreds of
youngsters, to the more subdued murmur of learning and teaching, to the total stillness when the students had gone home for
the day or were on holidays. In my mind's eye I also saw shadowy
figures from the past moving about: there was 'The Man', with
his slow shuffle; 'Lolly' (Brother Loyola), with his brisk, decisive
movements: Evangelist, with his long stride; Vincent with his
head held sideways; Dan Duggan, bustling with purposeful
stride; Con Buckley, clutching a briefcase and a huge bundle of
exercise copies; 'The Beet', with his portly but sedate movement;
Johnny Mahony, bowler-hatted, retreating round the corner to
the Western Road after his day's work. The memories merge into
a pattern because so many of these people were associated with

the College over a long period, giving it an atmosphere of unusual stability and continuity that makes recall easy. I found I was standing on the site where a circular wooden seat had been made around one of the few surviving tree stumps. Alas, there is now no trace of this seat or of the tree stumps: what secrets the smooth concrete surface of today hides!

The main entrance in my time was from the Western Road, where the trams were still noisily clanking and the high-pitched sound of their engines filled the air as they accelerated away from the stop. I well remember the 'Muskerry Dasher', in its station across the road: when it came to life in the afternoon we knew that our time of release was at hand. I often raced it on my bicycle out the Straight Road and it was a matter of pride to catch up with it at the Carrigrohane halt before parting company with it again, as I climbed the hill, past the old mill to my home in Ballincollig. My first introduction to schooling in the local national school had not been too successful and my poor mother, who was Principal of the girls' school, decided to send me to Pres, after many tears and nightmares. My brother, Tim, had already matriculated there. The change worked, and, escorted by an older friend, the late Pa Joe Ahern, subsequently a dentist, I settled to a routine, first as pupil and later as a teacher, that has given me a precious legacy of friendships and happy memories.

Even to someone as young as I was, though in no conscious manner, the tradition and atmosphere of Pres, was palpable. From its opening on the Western Road in 1888 the careers of two Brothers were synonymous with the running of the Junior and Senior Departments. From the old 'Lancs' on Lancaster Quay, Brother Ignatius Connolly, known always as 'The Man', brought many of his students to the new foundation and his connection with the College lasted until his death in 1944. I made closer contact with Brother Loyola ('Lolly'), who ruled the Junior School until his death in 1940. My first year or so was spent in the first floor of the second block, erected in 1901, with the old open-plan space where several classes and their teachers were accommodated. This, in itself, was a distracting and noisy arrangement, but, when the bedlam of traffic outside was added, you got challenging, if not difficult, teaching and learning conditions. Loyola was tall and vigorous as well as being an excellent disciplinarian. However, his innate kindness kept shining through. My abiding memory is of his tuition of me and a small group of three or four others who had missed the regular preparation for First Communion. We received special coaching in his little office off the Physics Laboratory. This little room was full of books, jotters, pens, nibs, jars of ink and cardboard boxes of purple school skull-caps, beautifully arranged according to size and wrapped in tissue paper. Our study of the small green Catechism was often interrupted by a customer for one of these items from his shop. One day I remember he sold a cap, shrewdly judging the size with a sharp glance at the customer's head, fitting it with a brisk precision, while not forgetting to collect payment at the end of the transaction. He was always doling out pennies for the bus, especially on wet days and, as a country boy – Ballincollig was then five miles west in the heart of the country – I was often the recipient of sixpence. He was always well groomed, with silver hair shining under the biretta that he and 'The Man' invariably wore. The space situation was improving rapidly and soon I was under Sebastian in No. 21 Dyke Parade, where new rooms and offices were being refurbished. I was taught by a Mr Franklin in Second Class and then by Michael and Nessan with Carthage Kelleher for my Confirmation year. By this time we were back in the old building which was now neatly partitioned into four classrooms. 'Lolly' seemed to be always present and active, stopping for a moment to talk, to ask about oneself and one's family, never delaying too long. Part of the kindly ambience of the place seemed to diminish with his death in 1940, and I remember with affection his practical, kindly and thorough teaching, his simple and direct spirituality, as he prepared us in that little office for first Communion, bringing us beforehand to a kindly Franciscan, Fr Oliver, in Broad Lane, to make our first Confession, without fear or embarrassment.

By the time I entered the Secondary Department, 'The Man' largely devoted his attention to the famous Bank Class to ensure that his staff – 'Doggy' Sheehan (memorably evoked by Seán Ó'Faoláin in *Vive Moi*), Johnny Mahony and Tim Donoghue ('Beetie') – could survive in some kind of order and impart a modicum of information and skills in that tough assignment. While Loyola was brusque and pragmatic, 'The Man' was gentler, small, red-apple cheeked, quietly spoken with a strong nasal accent and a tendency to preface every remark with 'Eh', his sternest term of opprobrium being, 'Eh! you're a great puppy'. He also had the ability to appear suddenly, surfacing out of the blue at some crisis point. He rambled from class to class giving little ten-minute pep talks, the content of which varied little over the years. I, too, in my turn, heard his tributes to Marshal Foch, 'a daily communicant, boys!' Like Loyola, he was devoted to Mary of the Presentation whose life and work provided an inspiring educational ideal and a living model for the daily task in hand.

Yet, there was a roguish realism about 'The Man', noticeable, for instance, in the twinkle in his eye. Over the years, I recall that, in his little ten-minute chats, he would commend the Rosary as the ideal form of prayer in the lower classes. Later, in the middle years, he would remark, 'Never forget to say a decade of the Rosary every day'. Finally, in the senior class, I can recall him telling us of a former pupil, now given to drink, in a remote outpost of the far-flung empire, never forgetting to say a single 'Hail Mary' every day. Eventually, *in extremis*, the required spiritual aid came just in time. 'Doggy' Sheehan always referred to 'The Man' as Mr Connolly, which, in itself, revives a memory of the old title of the Brothers, 'The Gentlemen of the Presentation'. In a prize I received for passing the Intermediate Certificate in 1942 (a copy of Corkery's *Stormy Hills*), he signed himself 'E. J. Connolly'. After the National University of Ireland conferred an honorary LLD on him for services to education, he was often affectionately referred to as 'The Doc'. Like Edmund Rice, he was acutely concerned about encouraging his pupils to develop a steady involvement with the less well-off, who lived in Sheare's Street, Crosses Green and the lanes off Barrack Street in the immediate environs of the College. He devoted himself to organising the School Conference of the St Vincent de Paul Society. He'd remind the members weekly, 'Eh, are you going to the Vincent de Paul tonight?' If, for any reason, you failed to attend, he would check with the Chairman, the late Pat Foley of Castle Street, and, next day, he would say, 'You weren't at the Vincent de

Paul last night. Make sure to be there next week'. He died in 1944 during my first year at the University, and I can still recall the palpable sense of loss and affection among all who were present at his funeral. With his complex brand of simplicity, warm humanity, scholarship and deep spirituality, he was a remarkable product of his time. His example and memory continue to inspire. The old moulds have been broken and too much has changed too fast.

Evangelist Griffin was another great influence. During his long career in the College he was a fine teacher and administrator. In his two long spells as Superior he ran the entire College from a well-filled wall press, packed with books and old examination papers and a black notebook that contained all the lists and information he required He had bushy eyebrows surmounting grey eyes that acquired the cutting power of a laser if he glared at you in anger or annoyance. He had odd speech inflections, ending sentences with propositional phrases like 'in it', or 'for it' or 'in connection with it'. His staff notices were famous. Of a Cup Match, 'If win, half-day; if not, classes as usual'.

He wasted neither words nor time and asked no one to do anything he was not prepared to do himself. His philosophy was 'Be there and keep them at it'. In Religious Instruction classes his speciality was Dr Sheehan's *Apologetics*, which was a storehouse of doctrine and relevant information, especially in the detailed footnotes and objections, which, I must confess, were often more cogently expressed and raised more hares than the main body of the text. Little foxed Evangelist, and the 'text', another great word of his, provided the answer. He often could not understand what was bothering someone. 'It's all in the text', he would say, and the comprehensive Sheehan suited his approach well. His shyness and basic reticence concealed a great concern and awareness. My widowed mother died in 1941, and, as a result, my scholastic performance disimproved considerably. Neither was it helped by changes that were happening in the range of school activities.

I was in the school unit of the LDF while Der Breen, myself and others had established a thriving drama group and were taking part in drama festivals. (Evangelist asked, 'Will there be girls in it?"); The Debating Society, founded some years earlier by

Brother Austin, had become a very lively force, and I also got my place on the College rugby team. Unlike students today, labouring zealously for points, I had a beatific sixth year, one of the best of my life from the standpoint of a general education. One day, towards the end of the last term, Evangelist and Vincent bore down on me and suggested that I enter the Scholarship Group, with a view to obtaining some kind of an scholarship or exhibition UCC. The College had always prided itself on getting a number of these awards annually in keeping with its high academic standards. They laid down the law and practically insisted that I attempt what then seemed to me the impossible. Their faith in my ability amazed me, but they also pointed out how welcome any cash input would be to my family in our fairly straitened circumstances. I never worked so hard and, to my own surprise, I succeeded. In the process I learned something that proved of benefit all through my life, that the trust and considered, dispassionate advice of good people, acting disinterestedly for the welfare of others, is a powerful motivating factor in achievement.

I am trying to convey by all this my awareness of a constant, caring atmosphere that formed part of the ambience of those days. It sprang from the dedication and spiritual resources which animated so many of my mentors and their sense of the long tradition to which they were heirs. It was the Feast of the Presentation on 21 November, always a school holiday, that focused my own understanding on the joint influence of Mary and Edmund Rice in the Order. It was an invariable practice that prior to the feast day, time would be given to this subject in religion classes. At one time I remember Brother Austin, who was doing some research into the Order and its efforts in the early years to provide popular education in Cork, talking about Brother Augustine Reardon and some of his companions, who, in the 1820s, preferred to carry on with the old Presentation model of Brotherhood rather than that of Jean Baptist De La Salle, which had been adopted in Mount Sion in Waterford. He had a strong feeling that Edmund Rice's role as co-founder of the twin congregations which stemmed from the original Presentation Society, needed to be retold and re-emphasized. It was also a fact that at least four of the lay staff in 'Pres.', had spent some time in the Christian Brothers and they certainly brought a dedication and sense of vocation to every aspect of their work there.

I had personal experience of the help and kindness of the staff when I returned to teach at my old school. So many of them were genuinely pleased that I had decided to follow my own family's long teaching tradition and my former teachers welcomed me as a colleague. At that time there were about ten lay staff and five or six Brothers in the Secondary Department. The camaraderie was great, the morale high and the spirit of co-operation, allowing for the inevitable tensions in any education establishment, extremely good. I continued with my dramatic work and with the Debating Society. Affected by the tenor and ethos of my training, it became the practice of the Presentation Theatre Guild to present a Passion play or a religious drama each year, preferably during Lent. The advantage was that you could usually use a fairly large cast and involve them in the experience of mounting a production. *Behold Your King, Caesar's Friend, The Trial of Christ* (presented in the old Opera House). *The Veil,* T.S. Eliot's *Murder in the Cathedral, The Strong are Lonely,* a fine play on the story of the Jesuit settlement in Paraguay, recently treated in the film *The Mission,* all come to mind. It would be difficult to present plays of this kind in these more secular times, but the Guild lasted independently until 1964, when it was gradually absorbed into the New Everyman movement.

Mention of *The Strong are Lonely* reminds me that we were also aware of the missionary work of the Order. Brothers came back from Canada and told us of the contrasting lifestyle and demands made on them in such differing conditions. 'Yankee Dan' (Brother Albertus Reen, RIP, who lived to reach his century) was a marvellous raconteur, who sometimes spent the greater part of his class periods regaling his eager listeners with reminiscences of his years in Canada, leading Dan Duggan, who had his class the following year, to remark, 'Ye know all about Montreal but not enough about Allen's *Latin Grammar*'. Big Brother Cassian too, often told us how he dealt with a blasphemous obscenity about the Mother of God: 'Off with the coat, boys! Off with the collar! Up with the fists! Laid him out boys, laid him out!' Looking at Cassian, his fine physique striking even in old age, we could well believe it.

I can also recall when Archbishop Finbarr Ryan visited, and I attended a public lecture in the Dairy Science Lecture Hall of UCC, where he talked of the educational needs in his archdiocese of Port of Spain in the West Indies. Many Brothers left to follow a new challenge, doing marvellous pioneer work which providentially had most welcome reciprocal benefits for Pres, itself. My final years in the old building were spent assisting, as Vice-Principal, two of that loyal band who spent many years abroad, Brothers Jerome and Bartholomew. Jerome in particular returned at a time when the College was somewhat in the doldrums. Times were changing and a fresh sense of direction and impulse were badly needed. Such a revitalizing energy could only come from outside. Re-organization and new structures provided the key motivating forces that were to transform the rather stodgy and static atmosphere and re-energise all of us, at the same time restoring the kind of prestige and dynamism the College formerly had. Again, Brother Jerome's strong social conscience, like that of 'The Man' of yore, led to the foundation and development of SHARE. Once more it was only fitting that history repeat itself when the National University of Ireland awarded him an honorary doctorate in recognition of his work. Subsequently, Cork Corporation gave him the Freedom of the City. It was a great privilege to serve with him and his successor, Bartholomew, who was to be my last Principal in the old building. The crowded conditions and the fact that the building had virtually become a traffic island led to some decisive thinking and action on his part. There was only one thing to be done: 'Seo chuige in ainm Dé'. In a spirit of complete faith and trust, albeit in indifferent health, and towards the end of a long, varied and useful career, he brought his building scheme to fruition and ensured a worthy building for the College into the next century.

With the transfer of the old Pres across the Mardyke to the ample space and facilities of the fine new complex, my memories come to an end. As I stand in the familiar site, still fully used and well-maintained by its present owners, UCC, I part company with all who laboured here for so long. When the traffic light turns green, I cross the wide thoroughfare of the present Mardyke, crammed with traffic flowing into Cork city from the west, and visualise it as it was when I first came here in 1932: a pleasant, tree-lined walk for pedestrians and cyclists only, flanked by the murky waters of the Dyke stream.

WE WILL NOT PLAY THE HARP BACKWARD* NOW, NO
Greg Delanty

If in Ireland they play the harp backward at need
Marianne Moore, 'Spenser's Ireland'

We, a bunch of greencard Irish,
        vamp it under the cathedral arches
        of Brooklyn Bridge that's strung like a harp.
But we'll not play
the harp backward now, harping on
        about those Micks who fashioned
this American wind lyre
and about the scores
        who landed on Ellis Island
or, like us, at Kennedy and dispersed
through this open sesame land

in different directions like the rays
        of Liberty's crown, each ray set
        against the other, forming a wedge or caret.
We'll refrain from inserting
how any of us craved for the old country
        and in our longing, composed a harp,
pipe, porter and colleen Tír na nÓg.
And if we play
        the harp right way round now
we'll reveal another side of the story
told like the secret of Labraid the exile: how

some, at least, found a native genius for union
        here and where like the Earl Gerald,
        who turned himself into a stag
and a green-eyed cat
of the mountain, many of us
        learned the trick
of turning ourselves into ourselves,

free in the Fe Fiada anonymity
     of America. Here
we could flap the horse's ears
of our singularity and not have to fear,
nor hide from the all-seeing Irish
     small town, blinking evil eyes –
     Nor does this landscape play that unheard,
but distinctly audible
mizzling slow air
     that strickens us with the plaintive notes
of the drawn-out tragedy
of the old country's sorry history.
     No, we'll not play the harp backward
anymore, keeping in mind the little people's harp
and how those who hear it never live long afterward.

* 'The harp is the symbol of Ireland. To play it backward is to be sentimental about the past'. Annotation to Moore's 'Spenser's Ireland' in
The Norton Anthology of Modern Poetry.

THE CONTRIBUTION OF PRES CORK TO RUGBY

Edmund Van Esbeck

Tradition has been defined as the transmission of long-established beliefs and customs handed down from generation to generation. It is, unquestionably, an important factor in the field of sporting endeavour and, indeed, in many elements of life and is a priceless asset.

Whenever people talk of the rugby prowess of successive generations who have worn the famous black and white jersey of Presentation Brothers College Cork invariably reference is made to the fact that the school has 'a wonderful rugby tradition' and so indeed it has. I believe it has been mutually beneficial to the school and to Irish rugby. The contribution to the game by Pres has been immense, the level of achievement without precedent in the annals of Munster rugby.

The traditions of any club or organisation are based on the efforts of countless people through the years and so it has been with Pres. This is not a history of rugby in the great academy of learning, rather a brief tribute to an element of life in the college that has been both vitally important and sustained over a period of one hundred years.

Like many an institution and organisation that has grown to eminence, in the rugby context the beginnings were humble. The famous school on the Western Road in Cork that backed out on to the Mardyke was founded in 1878. Its contribution to the educational and sporting life of Cork city has, in the interim, been immense and a host of pupils, my two late brothers and myself privileged to be among them, have reason to be grateful for what it gave us.

Many of those pupils later gained eminence in diverse fields of life, not alone in Cork and Ireland, but in faraway places. In the rugby context, which is my brief here, the roll of honour is impressive testimony to the distinction gained by former pupils of the college in the colours of Ireland and the Lions.

The game was first played in Pres in the closing years of the eighteen century, a period often referred to by our social historians as the gay nineties. Organisation in those days of the Victorian era was, to say the least, loose, and the early games were arranged on what might be termed an *ad hoc* basis. Aware of the need for organised competition, the Munster Branch decided to organise competitions between Cork colleges and so the Cork Senior and Junior Schools Cups came into being. Those competitions were to fashion the ongoing rivalry between Pres and Christian Brothers College in Cork.

The game was obviously prospering in the college in the late 1890s and, in fact, there is a record of Pres competing against club teams and in 1898 they entered a team for the Cork City and County Junior Cup, a competition that was contested by club teams. Pres reached the semi-final of the cup which was eventually won by Cork Constitution. Pres defeated a team called Ason's and then lost in the semi final to GPO.

When Pres won the Cork Senior Schools Cup in 1902/3, it set the trend for the future generations – how very well they have carried on the tradition of success. The following season Pres did the double, winning both the Cork Senior and Junior Cups.

In 1909 The Munster Branch started the Munster Schools Senior Cup and that great competition has adorned the rugby calendar ever since. In the early days of the century rugby was not the only game played in Pres and, indeed, the college enjoyed quite a deal of success in colleges hurling. But playing both hurling and rugby probably took its toll and imposed excessive demands and eventually the college concentrated on rugby.

A great day in the history of the college came in 1918 when Pres won the Munster Senior Schools Cup for the first time under the captaincy Charlie Nolan. Two years later Charlie Haly, whose son Michael and grandsons subsequently played with distinction for the college, led the second Pres team to win the Munster Cup. While there was success in other competitions it was not until 1927 that Pres won the Munster Cup for the third time under the leadership of Tim O'Driscoll. In the early days of the competition it was Rockwell and CBC who were the most successful colleges, but Pres won the trophy three times in the 1930s.

In 1933 the Munster Branch extended schools competition by starting a Munster Schools Junior Cup and, after Limerick CBS won the inaugural competition, Pres won the trophy in 1934 and the man who led the side to victory was Pat Barry, a legendary figure in the annals of rugby in Pres.

The second half of the 1940's was a very successful era for the college. The Munster Senior Cup was won in 1945 and for the first time retained by Pres in 1946. Dan Coughlan led the 1945 side to success and the late Noel Nunan captained the 1946 winning team. Those two seasons were especially memorable and productive for the Munster Junior Cup was also won both years. Thus, 1945 was the first year that Pres did the big double of Senior and Junior Cups.

I was a young pupil at the college in those years and have vivid memories of the excitement that obtained in the school as the famous 'Tango!' was chanted when the trophies were carried around each classroom for the acclamation of the heroes who had brought such honour to the school.

A man who contributed a great deal in the thirties was Brother Berchmans Boyce, as kindly a man as one could wish to meet. Freddy Holland, a distinguished maths teacher, made a considerable contribution to those wins in the 1940s and Pat Barry was called in to lend his expertise and enthusiasm. Brother Vincent was also deeply involved then and for many years subsequently.

When Pres won the senior cup in 1935, a member of the side was hooker Charlie Teehan and there was great celebration and delight when Charlie was picked to play for Ireland in 1939. The production line of Irish internationals from Pres had started.

Five times between 1948 and 1958 Pres won the Munster Senior Cup and the Junior Cup was won three times in that period as well. Some of the players who helped fashion those victories went an to attain the highest honours in the game. The man who led the senior team to cup success in 1952 was Tom Nesdale and he, too, was capped for his country. Prop Mick O'Callaghan, who was on the 1954 cup-winning side, was another international. Liam Coughlan, who also played on that side, was extremely unlucky not to attain the ultimate honour, having played in several final Irish trials. Jerry Murray was a member of the 1958 cup-winning team and another who played in several final trials without gaining a cap, but he was honoured by the Barbarians and subsequently became a distinguished member of the Ireland selection committee.

When Ireland did the Grand Slam in 1948 and won the Triple Crown and championship in 1949, a former Pres boy, Bertie O'Hanlon, was on the side. Bertie had, however, gone to Rockwell after his early years in Pres and it was in the colours of Rockwell that he made a mark an schools rugby.

Pres won the Munster Schools Junior Cup in 1954 and the team was led by the late Jerry Walsh. He later became a great Ireland centre and played for the Lions, but it was another member of the 1954 Junior Cup team, Tom Kiernan, who was to emerge as the most distinguished of all former Pres internationals. Tommy was capped a record fifty-four times for Ireland and captained his country on twenty-four occasions, a record unequalled in the annals of Irish rugby. He went on to captain the Lions on the tour to South Africa in 1968. At coaching and administrative levels he scaled heights of equal distinction. He became President of the Munster Branch and subsequently of the IRFU. As a coach he also enjoyed immense success. He coached the Munster team to a famous victory over the All Blacks in 1978 and in 1982 was coach when Ireland won the Triple Crown, their first such success since 1949. Nor has his contribution finished as he is currently one of Ireland's representatives on the International Rugby Board.

When Pres won the Munster Senior Cup in 1966 the team was led by Barry McGann who went on to fashion a great international career. He is still rated as one of the greatest of all schools rugby players. One of his team mates on that side, scrum half Donal Canniffe, was another to play for his country and it was Canniffe who captained the Munster side that defeated the All Blacks in 1978. A very sad footnote to the win in 1966 was that Pat Barry died suddenly on the evening of the match. His contribution had been immense, his dedication to rugby in the college total. Pres won the Senior Cup three times in the 1960s but were even more successful in the Junior Cup, its five wins in that decade including a truly remarkable four in row between 1963 and 1966.

In that period the involvement of such as Brothers David, Athanasius and Felim and subsequently Brothers Placid, Fergal and John Beecher were of considerable importance. Declan Healy and the late Finbarr Harrington also made significant contributions in the 1960s and 1970s as did the late Des Barry, brother of Pat, before his untimely death while engaged in a training session with the school. He was succeeded by Flor O'Sullivan, Noel Murphy and Finbarr Pope.

In more recent times Declan Kidney, a man who had known the glory of cup victory while a pupil at the school, then made a huge contribution to coaching and his expertise in that area found expression when he was appointed coach to the Ireland schools side. He had an able ally in Pat Attridge, who, when Declan had to stand aside to pursue further study, took over as coach. Pat, like Declan had attained cup success while a student at Pres and they knew the tradition: the heritage was in safe hands. Pat Attridge was the man who guided the side to victory in April of this year (1996) when Pres won the Senior Cup for the twenty-fifth time, the first school to achieve that very significant milestone.

But I run slightly ahead of my time. While the junior cup was won four times in the 1970s, Pres had a comparatively lean period by their standards at senior level in that decade although still producing some fine players. The Senior Cup was won in 1975 and 1978. The win in 1975 coincided with the centenary season of the IRFU. To mark that occasion it was decided that Ireland would field a team at schools international level for the first time and Pres had no fewer than three players on the team that played England in March 1975 at Lansdowne Road. They were Moss Finn, later to win many caps for Ireland at senior level, Jimmy Bowen, another man to achieve the ultimate distinction, and Brian Clifford. Once in the international arena at schools level, schools internationals became a regular feature and Pres has sent out a host of youngsters who have been capped at schools level.

A youngster who played on the junior cup winning team of 1978 was Michael Kiernan, nephew of Tom and son of Jim, who, himself, was a fine player for the school and later became an Ireland selector. Michael gained schools international caps, went on to be capped at senior level and was on the Ireland teams that won Triple Crowns in 1982 and 1985. He had a great career that included selection for the Lions and he also holds the record for points scored for Ireland with an unmatched 308.

Like the 1970s, the senior cup was won twice in the 1980s and scrum half on the team that won in 1981 under Ray Clarke's captaincy was Michael Bradley. He was at that time on the foothills of a great career that saw him gain caps at schools level and then go on to be part of Ireland's Triple Crown winning side of 1985 alongside Michael Kiernan. Michael Bradley became the most capped scrum half in Ireland's rugby history and, like Tom Kiernan, was honoured with the captaincy of his country.

In the 1980s Pres won the Junior Cup no fewer than six times including four in a row between 1983 and 1986. One of the players who helped in those successes and led the team to victory in the Senior Cup of 1987 was Ken O'Connell, who went on to play for his country first at schools and later at senior level.

There is no doubt but that the decade of the 1990s has been the most productive and successful in the history of the college. The Senior Cup has been won five times between 1991 and 1996, with a win for Crescent over Pres in the final in 1994 being the only break in the sequence. The Junior Cup was won in 1992 and for the twenty-fourth time in 1995 when Pres did the double yet again.

So, twenty-five senior cups and twenty-four Junior Cups as well as many victories in other competitions such as the Bowen Shield and the now defunct Cork Senior and Junior Cups are telling testimony to the ongoing quality of the game of rugby in Presentation College, Cork. The old academy on the Western Road is now no more as a splendid new building was erected on the old school playing-fields on the Mardyke some years ago and the rugby activity moved to a new location in Wilton. It had all started on a piece of ground adjacent to the Brothers' residence at Mardyke House.

The roll of honour is long and distinguished both in collective achievement and on an individual basis. The list of former Pres boys who have been capped for Ireland at senior level would make up a very formidable side. Charlie Teehan set the trend and there followed Bertie O'Hanlon, Michael Bradley, Jimmy Bowen, Donal Canniffe, Jimmy Corcoran, Marney Cunningham, Moss Finn, Ralph Keyes, Tom Kiernan, Michael Kiernan, Barry McGann, Paul McCarthy, Tom Nesdale, Mick O'Callaghan, Ken O'Connell, Archie O'Leary and Jerry Walsh.

A few more came very close and one thinks of such as Jack Guiney and Eddie O'Mullane, a great scrum half for the school in the 1930s. They both played for Irish XVs during the 1939-45 war when internationals were suspended and caps were not awarded. Another was Tommy Moroney, rated by some as the greatest of all schools rugby players. He went on to a great career in soccer and gained a host of international caps, as did another former pupil, Liam O'Neill. Derry Crowley, a fine hooker, toured Argentina and Chile with Ireland in 1952 but did not gain a full cap and then there were Jerry Murray and Liam Coughlan who came so very close.

As I write this small tribute to a wonderful contribution, the Ireland schools side is preparing to tour Australia. There are two Pres boys in the squad, Tim Cahill, who captained the side that won the Senior Cup last March, and Peter Stringer. They are carrying on a wonderful tradition. Let those who follow be inspired by the deeds of those sung and unsung heroes who learned their rugby in Pres and then went on to rugby eminence. I feel sure that tradition will be maintained and that we will hear the victory 'Tango' many times in the years to come.

A JEWISH BOY GOES TO PRES

Cecil Hurwitz

In the Autumn of 1932, I, Cecil Hurwitz, a Jewish boy, almost six years old, entered the gates of Presentation College, on the Western Road ('Pres.'), to begin my formal education at the 'Prep' school.

I was born in Cork of Orthodox Jewish parents, though my father came to Ireland with his family from Lithuania at the turn of the century. He was then only six years old and his family settled in Cork. My mother, who was born in Dublin, later came to Cork with her parents, who had also emigrated from Lithuania. As the Jewish population in Cork was relatively small (a maximum of 100 families), it was not financially viable to establish a Jewish school there. Today, sad to state, there are only a handful of Jewish people in the Cork area.

The options, therefore, for the education of Jewish children were twofold. Parents had a choice to send their children either to Catholic schools or Protestant schools. It must be pointed out, however, that, at the time, very few schools accepted Jewish children as pupils, and it is to the eternal credit of the Presentation Brothers that they enrolled Jewish boys in their school on the Western Road.

In the 1930s, ecumenism was not a word in common usage. The Presentation Brothers were ecumenists long before that word became fashionable. I owe them a great debt of gratitude, because, in later life, I became very much involved in the ecumenical movement, when I spearheaded the promotion of prayer for peace and reconciliation in Ireland.

Another plus where the Pres Brothers and their lay teachers were concerned, was their insistence that the religious beliefs of minority pupils be safeguarded and protected. So, during the times allotted for religious instruction, Jewish pupils left the classroom to spend that half hour in a cloakroom, studying the text-book of the subject next on the timetable.

But, in spite of these precautions, I came face to face with Jesus Christ in a cloakroom on a day that is indelibly printed on my mind, thus beginning a long process which led me, inexorably, from Synagogue to Church.

The Diocesan Inspector was doing his rounds, and Pres was preparing for his arrival. The teachers were busy ensuring that their charges knew the answers to the Catechism questions, and were familiar with the arguments in apologetics and prescribed Scripture stories. The students had, also, to be word-perfect when reciting the prayers in Irish as well as English.

I, of course, had a tremendous amount of free time, as I left the classroom to go to a nearby cloakroom to study my text-books. Now this solitary confinement, though possibly welcome to others, was not only boring to me, but, because I was cooped up in a small space, had a claustrophobic effect upon me.

On this particular day I entered the cloakroom with my book clutched in my hand, and, as I perused a poem, endeavouring to memorise it, my eyes alighted on a book on the floor. I vividly recall picking it up and saying to myself that this book had to be more interesting than the poem I was trying to memorise. It was one of the Gospels, and I read for the first time the story of Jesus, as told by the Gospel writer, from crib to tomb. When I read of the arrest, passion and crucifixion of this wonderful man, and the role played by my people in his execution, I found myself falling on my knees, and, with tears falling from my eyes, I made my first profession of faith in Jesus Christ as my God. It was truly significant that I found myself on my knees, because Jewish people do not kneel in worship.

In trying to safeguard my religious beliefs, the Brothers did not reckon with God when he decides to plant the seeds of Faith in the minds of those he chooses. 'You have not chosen me', Jesus said, 'but I have chosen you'. Many years were to elapse, and many roads would be travelled before I finally received the water of baptism at the Dominican Church in Cork on the vigil of Pentecost 1949. I was then a twenty-two-year-old Pentecost baby. The full story is told in my autobiography, *From Synagogue to Church* (Pauline Publications, Cork). Never, ever, will I forget that memorable day in a blessed cloakroom in Pres when Jesus

Christ made himself known to me and called me to be his disciple and follower.

Every schoolboy has memories of his schooldays. The teachers who were dreaded, and those who were liked, the intense rivalry that existed among the players and the supporters of opposing schools on the rugby pitch. The 'Tango', with its meaningless words, that truly warmed the cockles of our hearts, as the Munster Senior and Junior Cups were raised in triumph. The lunch-room was then presided over by Denis Buckley, who cheered us up no end when he told us that we were getting a half-day, then mischievously adding the rider – at 4.00 p.m!

The faces of the teachers come vividly to mind. One begins, of course, with Dr. E.J. Connolly ('The Man'), a truly wonderful educationalist, who recruited, in his day, many Pres boys for the Indian (did I hear him correctly? I thought he said 'Injun'!) Civil Service.

Then there was Brother Evangelist. 'Slat', we used to call him. Nearly every teacher had a nickname. 'Where is my slat?' he used to say. We knew, of course, that this was just a threat, or even a mannerism of speech. There was Brother Cassian ('Casha'), who taught us Maths. Even though he was a Maths teacher, Brother Cassian was very meticulous about the use of the English language. A pupil might say, '2 over 4', and he would be immediately corrected, 'Never say that! You must say 2 divided by 4'. To emphasise his point, he would say that the ceiling is over the floor, but it is not divided by the floor. Johnny (Réidh) Dorgan was our Irish teacher. 'Réidh é' (settle down) was a phrase he frequently used in the classroom. Florrie McCarthy ('Macker') taught us History and Geography. Brother Austin Queenan gave me a love for the works of William Shakespeare. Kevin ('Bevel') Harty was the Art teacher (I couldn't draw a straight line with a ruler).

Connie ('Pug') Buckley was another Irish teacher. Johnny Mahony, who married late in life, was also on the staff, as well as the much loved Tim ('The Beet') Donoghue. In the Chemistry class Paddy ('Ikey') O'Reilly presided. I always wanted to know why Mr O'Reilly was dubbed 'Ikey'? One day, my brother-in-law told me the story.

Eric Scher, another Jewish student, dozed off to sleep in Mr O'Reilly's class, and was duly spotted. For the life of him, Paddy

O'Reilly could not remember Eric's name. He shouted at Eric, 'Wake up, Ikey!' Strange as it may seem, the boys never called Eric 'Ikey'. That dubious title was reserved for the Chemistry teacher instead.

Mr Paddy Gerraghty ('The Ger') also taught Maths. I understand that 'The Ger' was himself, a pupil of Pádraig Pearse's famous and historic school (Scoil Éanna), in Dublin. No reminiscences of Pres teachers in the 1930s and 1940s would be complete without mentioning the human tornado, Danny Duggan – 'D Squared', the pupils named him. Danny never walked into a room. He seemed to burst into it, almost detaching the hinges from the door, and, as he strode across the room to his desk, he barked out, 'Books closed, please' and then began to examine us in the prescribed texts as well as Longman's and Allen's Latin grammar. If we didn't know it, we were required to write it out. Then we made sure never to make such a silly mistake again. Danny had a justifiable boast, 'If Danny Duggan can't teach you, nobody else can'. We certainly knew our Latin, and I developed a great love for the language, thanks mainly to Danny Duggan. If I could fault Danny at all (and this had nothing to do with Latin), it was for his inability to pronounce my name. 'Hurtz', he called me.

All in all, I spent eleven years in Pres., and they were memorable and happy ones. I owe a great deal to all my teachers. I will always remember, with deep emotion, that it was in Presentation College, that the first seeds of my Catholic faith were sown in an insignificant cloakroom.

Every school has its special ethos, and Pres is no exception. Most students will probably speak of the Christian values inculcated by the Brothers and lay teachers, in the course of fostering character formation and the development of personality. And this undoubtedly took place in Pres. But for me, a Jewish boy, there was something else, something special for me. This was the fact that the Brothers and lay teachers in Pres taught me a wonderful lesson in tolerance. The spirit of ecumenism which they demonstrated in Cork of the 1930s and 1940s was truly remarkable. By accepting pupils from a different religious persuasion, they showed Catholics and Jews alike that there was no room for bigotry at Presentation College. Jesus said, 'Love one another, as I have loved you', and the Pres Brothers took that axiom very much to heart.

In Northern Ireland, where there is so much bigotry, they could learn an invaluable lesson from the Presentation Brothers. Intolerance leads to injustice, which in turn leads to violence, and we know that in Northern Ireland violence has led to over three thousand people being killed and more than thirty-five thousand injured in body, mind and spirit.

May God bless the Presentation Brothers and their lay colleagues, and may the students under their care develop a great love for their alma mater, that seat of unquenchable learning – Presentation College, Cork.

ROSES FOR THE PRESIDENT
Patrick Galvin

You may recall, Mr President,
The incident in the square.
Perhaps, you would tell us about that.

When I die, the President declared,
Lay me out in the garden
So that I may taste the roses.
I have always been partial to roses
And once knew a girl
Who wore nothing else.

I have forgotten her name
And I have no memory for faces
But I do remember the roses.

As to the incident in the square,
Which you have mentioned many times,
I have no recollection of that.
It was probably raining
And people protest, largely,
Because of the vagaries in the weather.

The roses smelled sweet
I remember that –
And she was remarkably tall.

Of course, that particular incident
May not have taken place at all.
So many things are illusory –
The keening of snow
The endless dreamings of the heart.

She lay face down in the rain
The roses covered her
I remember that.

DISCOVERING A THIRST FOR LEARNING

Sean Maher

(From *The Road to God Knows Where*, 1972)

I eventually reached St Joseph's School in Cork city; I was, for an instant, disappointed. At first sight it was a large, dismal looking, red-brick building. Even when I entered its polished hallway I wasn't impressed; on meeting the Superior, however, I was. Behind a polished desk sat a very kindly looking greyhaired man, who spoke in a gentle voice.

'So you are the young gentleman who longs to be at school', he said to me.

'Yes sir,' I said timidly.

'Good,' said the Superior, 'but I would like you to call me "Brother", as do all the boys here. First of all, young man, I suppose it's only proper that I know your name, then we will be the wiser for our manners.'

'My name is Sean Devine, s... I mean Brother,' I said

'Sean Devine,' said the Superior. 'Well Sean, you should like our school and I hope very much that you will be happy here. What is your age, by the way? I've got all the other details here, but not your age.'

'I'm nine,' I lied.

'Oh, you are big for your age,' said the Superior. 'I suppose you don't know the date of your birth?'

'No Brother,' I said, 'I only know that I was nine last January.'

'Oh well, never mind, this will not be difficult to find out. Now, let Michael Alken here show you to the dining room. In fact, Michael, you can show Sean all around the school and be his guide and helper until he gets used to us. Do you understand, Michael?'

'Yes, Brother,' said the boy who had walked into the study.

'Very well then; now Sean, meet Michael who will be your guide and help you to get used to our school routine. He will verse you well, so don't be frightened to ask him questions, or me for that matter. We are here to help you, always remember this; you can both go now.'

'Thank you, Brother,' I said, and left the study with my guide, Michael Alken. 'Know-all', I was to learn later, was his nickname. I had taken an instant liking to Michael, who was nine years old. He looked very studious for his age. He brought me to the dining-room and to the table where he sat.

'This will be your table, Sean, for all your meals; you can sit next to me, because I am monitor. In fact I shall be your monitor whilst you remain at this table,' said Michael.

'Monitor? What's that?' I asked.

'Oh, that means a person in charge. You see,' Michael explained, 'every table has a monitor; as you can see there are eight boys to each table and one boy is appointed as monitor by the superior.'

'Oh,' I said, 'I see.'

'Anyway,' said Michael, 'you'll soon get the hang of it.'

Besides Michael, there were six other boys at my table, who all had nick-names, they were: Barracha, Tags, Busang, Tomato Jack, Lame Duck and Bucka. They were all around the same age as Michael, between nine and ten. I was very struck by the nick-names and even years afterwards I did not know some of the boys by their real names. In fact nearly everyone in the school had a nick-name, including the teachers. I was soon to learn all of them, and a lot more besides.

For the first week or so I did not go to class at all but spent my time going around the whole building with Michael, meeting all the Brothers and getting to know the whole place.

I got on with – and liked – Michael very well; in fact, within days, we became the best of friends and were to remain so for the duration of the time I was at St Joseph's. As we got to know each other I asked Michael loads and loads of questions.

'Where do you come from, Michael?'

'From Waterford. I have been here three years now. I go home for six weeks holidays each summer. You'll be able to go home too.'

'I don't think so,' I said, 'you see my parents don't live in a house – they are travellers.'

'Oh,' said Michael, in surprise.

I will always remember Michael Alken's 'Oh' of surprise when he first learned that my parents were travellers. It has typified, for me, Irish people's attitude towards us pavvies. We are different, not by creed or colour but by an indefinable something with which settled people have not come to terms. Michael knew that his reply had hurt me and tried to make amends:

'I didn't know that, but allow me to tell you not to say it to any of the other boys here because, if you do, they will kick you and you won't like it. I don't mind myself, but you'll do well to take my advice. Say you live anywhere, but not on the road.'

Thus I had to get used to being a boy from a respectable way of life rather than the more humble abode by the roadside. It sounded simple at first, but as the weeks went by I found it a strain until, with the help of a new-found friend, I soon got used to, and even mastered the difficulty.

Another acute embarrassment that I had to overcome was the start to my education, and this proved the most difficult of all. I could not read or write one single word when I arrived at St Joseph's School in Cork. So, to begin my schooling, I had to start in the infants' class. This, of course, meant being called 'baby' by the other boys in the school. Outwardly I did not seem to mind, but inwardly I felt the hurt of it. Luckily enough, I had a good ally in the form of Brother Columba, or 'Left Law', as he was known by the boys.

Brother Columba taught infants and first standard in the one large classroom and when he got a big lad like me – I was really twelve years old – he was presented with a problem. Unwittingly, however, I, in the end, was to become my own succour though I did not realise it at the time. It all began at a singing lesson one day when I was asked by Brother Columba why I wasn't joining in. I told the Brother quite innocently:

'I don't like the songs they sing in this school, Brother, they're not nice, especially the foolish Irish one about the boat in the sea.'

'Oh,' said Brother Columba calmly, 'and, pray minstrel, have you a better song to sing for us?'

'Of course I know better songs,' I said proudly, 'I know plenty that's better.'

'Then,' said the Brother, 'perhaps you will sing some of these better songs of yours, because we would love to hear them.'

'All right then, I'll sing the "Wild Colonial Boy" first', I said.

> There was a wild Colonial boy, Jack Duggan was his name,
> He was born and reared in Ireland, in a place called
>   Castlemaine,
> He was his father's only pride, his mother's pride and joy,
> And dearly did his parents love
>   the Wild Colonial Boy.

After singing this song everyone clapped and I was asked to sing another. Which I did.

> I don't give a damn, for gaiging is the best,
> For when a feen is corrped, sure he has a little rest.
> Sure he's got a little molly and he's got a little beor
> And it's off on the tober, with his molly and his beor.
>
> By night around the glimmer, when the gallias are'n lee
> You can see him dance a merry step a' there for you'n me.
> He doesn't have to worry and he doesn't have to care,
> So long as he's got a sark for his old grey mare.

This song had them all puzzled, because the words of it were quite strange. When I was asked if I knew the meaning of the words, I said I didn't. I knew that if I did so I would have to explain a lot of things besides the words of the song. The song in ordinary words goes as follows:

> I don't give a damn, for beggin' is the best.
> For when a man is tired, sure he has a little rest.
> Sure he's got a little tent and he's got a little woman,
> And it's off on the road, with his tent and his woman.
>
> By night around the fire, when the children are in bed,
> You can see him dance a merry step for either you or me.
> He doesn't have to worry and he doesn't have to care,
> So long as he's a field for his old grey mare.

These songs went down well with everyone in the classroom, and when I told the stories about the ghosts, on another occasion, I was even more popular. I told the story of the cats in the graveyard and others I had heard on the road.

I became part of the school in no time. I was accepted by the other boys there, without the usual reception that is set aside for boys who enter St Joseph's for the first time. I had, of course, to learn to adjust myself to a way and routine of life that was completely alien to me. I was gravely handicapped by my lack of any type of previous schooling, but, as if by a miracle, by the time I was six months at the school I was able to read and write fluently. The method of teaching practised at the school was, in my opinion when I first started, silly, and I said this too, to Brother Columba. The following week, however, I was put in another class where I was given a new school reader. The teacher in second class was Brother Theobald.

When he started reading the book to the class I fell in love with it straight away. In it were stories of Setanta, Fionn McCumhaill, Cuchulainn, The Fate of the Children of Lir and others. Here at last was my world, and the moment I heard them I was learning, and did not look back.

Within a short time I was moved up another standard, to third class, under the guidance of Brother Eugene. There is no doubt that it was the book of stories that created my interest for learning. Somehow the tales of Setanta, Tír-na-nÓg and that seemed very familiar to me. Somewhere I had heard these tales before, when I was on the road. Only the characters were different.

Brother Eugene was a man of fifty who had spent thirty or so of those years in the Order of the Presentation Brothers. He was different from the other Brothers in that he spoke with an English accent. He never taught Irish or singing, which made me quite happy. He was a man who loved English literature, and was forever telling stories and reading. Brother Eugene first became interested in me one day when he recited a poem by Longfellow to the class.

'Today,' Brother Eugene said, 'we are going to recite "The Village Blacksmith" by Henry Wadsworth Longfellow. I want to know whether you like it or not, and most important, *why* you like or dislike it.' After reciting the first verse of the poem, Brother Eugene asked if any boy in the class had heard the poem before.

'Yes, Brother,' I said, 'I could say that first verse easy.'

'Why, did you learn it before then?' asked the Brother.

'No Brother, but I like it cause I used to know lots of black-smiths.'

'Well, in that case, let's hear you reciting the first verse,' said the Brother.

> Under a spreading chestnut tree the village smithy stands,
> The smith, a mighty man is he, with large and sinewy hands,
> The muscles of his brawny arms are as strong as iron bands,
> His hair is crisp, black and long and his face is like the tan,
> And he looks the whole world in the face for he owes not any man.

'Are you sure,' asked the Brother, 'that you never learned this before?'

'Yes, Brother, I am sure that was the first time I ever heard it, but I do like it,' I answered.

When I sat down, the whole class was as silent as night, and all eyes were glued on me.

'Now, suppose I were to read out the whole poem to you, do you think you would be able to do the same, reciting it all.'

'I don't know', I said. 'I expect I could; at least I could try.'

Brother Eugene read out the three verses from the book. When he had finished, I walked up to the front of the class and recited the whole poem, word for word. Brother Eugene was amazed at my performance and was not slow in letting the whole class know it.

'This is very good for you, Sean,' he said. Then, to the class, he said, 'Isn't he very good, boys?' The whole class answered 'yes' in unison.

From that day on, Brother Eugene was to take an exceptional interest in me and develop my gift of learning. I loved every moment of the lessons I received from him for, whilst most of the boys in my class were still learning their ABC, I was delving into the classics under his guidance. In point of fact, Brother Eugene began teaching me after school, in the library. It was at such times that I could pour out questions without hindrance from my fellow classmates. Here too, in private, I was able to talk to him about road life and about my hatred of it.

At one of these sessions Brother Eugene said to me, 'Sean, you are a very remarkable boy. You have an unquenchable thirst for learning. Can you tell me why?'

'Oh, because I like it,' said I, 'particularly your stories, although some of the stories you tell are different than the ones I heard at home.'

'And how do you mean "different" Sean?', asked Brother Eugene.

'Ah, like St Patrick and that. You never tell about him being a traveller, like I was told on the road.'

'That is because you may have heard a false version', said Brother Eugene.

'No, it was not false, it's the one in the schoolbook that's wrong, because St Patrick was a travelling man,' I replied.

'With Irish history, English, Danish and what have you, perhaps yours is not false after all. There is one thing I want you to do, Sean, and that is to tell me some more of your stories about the past, the ones you have heard around the camp fires I mean. Will you do that?'

'Yes, Brother,' I said, 'I will tell you lots if you want me to.'

Thus I continued my questions. After the first year in school I had mastered reading, and in so doing read very widely about Ireland and its religious and literary history.

'Brother,' I said to my favourite teacher one day, 'in all the history books I have read of Ireland and England, there is never a word mentioned about the travellers.'

'Maybe', said the Brother politely, 'there were no travellers then.'

'Oh, but there were', I said. 'Even St Patrick used to travel with them, as well as the monks and the priests.'

'Yes, Sean, this may have been so, but the history of any country is very hard to pinpoint, especially that of many centuries ago. You must always remember that there were not many educated men in those days and you have to be very well educated to write any history.'

'This isn't true,' I said. 'Nearly every famous writer or poet of the past had hardly any education.'

'And who, may I ask you, told you that?' asked the Brother.

'Oh, a very old friend of mine on the road; he was old too, so he should know,' I answered.

'Well, to a certain extent, I suppose I shall have to grant you that.'

School for me was a godsend. I enjoyed every day I spent there, mostly for the learning. Reading books was my earthly heaven. 'All's well that ends well'; alas, with me this was never to be. Soon, like a cork, I was to be tossed out on the ocean of life, I was to be pared, as is the wattle, to support the rigging pole – to become, in other words, a cog in the wheel.

I could not voice against this for to do so was like the clucking hen voicing the linnet. To the tober I was born, and to the tober I must return.

It was on a bright March day in 1948 that I left St Joseph's Industrial School in Cork to return once more to the road. A week or two previous to my leaving, my father came to collect me. However, over a mistake in my age, he had to return home to get my birth-certificate. According to the school records I was only thirteen years old while my father, who was right, claimed I was sixteen.

When I arrived at the station at Dara after my long journey from Cork, I was greeted by a much older mother, a mother with a haggard face. Her lonely eyes were misted with tears, as were mine.

'Oh son,' she said, 'you have changed, but it's lovely to see you.'

'You have changed too, Mammy,' I said, 'but why the tears?'

'Oh, Alannah, I'm happy that's all,' she said.

SCHOOLDAYS: A TIME OF GRACE

John McGahern

A secondary school was opened by the Brothers in the town. The word *Salamanca*, having endured for most of a century as a mighty ball booted on the wind out of defence in Charlie's field, grew sails again on an open sea, became distant spires within a walled city in the sun. Race memories of hedge schools and the poor scholar were stirred, as boys, like uncertain flocks of birds, on bicycles, came long distances from the villages and outlying farms to grapple with calculus and George Gordon and the delta of the River Plate.

This description of the Presentation Brothers opening a secondary school in Carrick-on-Shannon in 1947 from the story 'Old-fashioned' is slanted into a fictional narrative that is rooted in fact. Our football field belonged to Charlie Reegan; it was directly behind his bar/grocery in the village, close to the banks of the Boyle River. The visiting teams changed in the bar. The local team, St Michael's, always changed in Charlie's empty or half-empty hayshed, draping their Sunday suits over the tedders or mowing machines or carts. I don't think we ever had a winning team. Most of our football was played out of defence. Whenever an enormous relieving clearance was booted down the field on the wind, a hopeful shout of *Salamanca!* would scatter from the sidelines.

Much later I learned that during the Penal Laws the boys who had vocations from our part of the country travelled to Spain by foot and horseback and fishing-boat to study for the priesthood in Salamanca. Words, like people, sometimes have to travel about in disguise and double for something other than what they are, and for a long time Salamanca has stood for me as a symbol of the outer limits of the North Roscommon imagination, which is no mean leap.

At that time people lived very much within the walls of their own small, local worlds. We knew very little about the big towns or what went on there. Boyle and Carrick were our towns, both of them six or seven miles away. I did not know the Brothers had started a secondary school a year before until one day, around Easter, Brother Damien came on his bicycle. I was planting potatoes with my father on Cox's Hill. I can still see Brother Damien lean his bicycle against the stone wall and come towards us across the field. He was dark and could have passed for a Spaniard, and later, when I was attending his school, he gained a certain reputation for reading an Italian newspaper each week. Reputations of all kinds fastened easily to people in those days. He told us that he was a Presentation Brother, that they had opened a secondary school for boys in Carrick-on-Shannon and that they were looking for pupils. They were offering six scholarships at their entrance exam in June. I sat the exam that year and won a half scholarship: it was worth four pounds a year for five years. I attended Presentation College, Carrick-on-Shannon from 1948 to 1953.

At that time secondary schooling was available only to the well-off and a few specially coached, academically bright students. The well-off and the lucky few attended Summerhill College or the Ursuline Convent in Sligo, thirty miles away, but the county town of Carrick had two secondary schools for boys as well as the Marist Convent for girls. I believe this to be entirely due to a Mrs Lynch, who must have been a remarkable woman for her time. A few years before she had started the Rosary High School, which offered commercial secretarial training to girls as well as secondary schooling to boys. A married woman in charge of a school of adolescent boys and girls must have set off all kinds of ecclesiastical alarms. I believe the Brothers were brought in to close her down. They didn't succeed. In fact, both schools got on well together. The result was that the poor hinterland of Carrick had one of the most open and competitive secondary school systems at a time when such schooling was kept strictly within the domain of the privileged.

The College was in a wing of the monastery. It had once been a military barracks. The community of Brothers lived in the other wing. They never numbered more than six or seven, and were made up of Brothers who taught at the long established national school on the hill as well as those from the College. The closest Presentation community was forty miles away in Enniskillen. I suspect the little community in Carrick had a great deal of freedom for that time.

Like all other boys from the country and outlying towns and villages, I cycled to school. The bicycles were stacked in the large downstairs room. The roads were poor. Most lunchtimes some boys could be seen with bicycles upside down in the big room, mending punctures. This room was between the sanded yard where we played soccer with a tennis ball and the handball alley at the back. Buckled wheels or broken chains had to be taken to Gill's Bicycle Shop across the road. At lunchtime there was always a race downstairs from classes to claim places in the alley. Often on dry evenings we'd stay behind after school to play handball before heading on our bicycles into the country and towards our main meal of the day.

The rough cement floor of the alley was ruinous on boots and shoes. Usually we played with the little 'Elephant' ball, but sometimes sponge and tennis balls had to serve instead. The 'Elephants' were expensive. Wild strokes would send them straying off the netting into the scrapyard of Gill's Garage. There, Aggie Gill was our scourge as she chased or tried to apprehend us while we searched among the scrapped cars and lorries and engine blocks and radiators for the precious little brown 'Elephant'.

Our lunches were carried with our bag of books, strapped or tied on the bicycle carriers: a bottle of milk with a few sandwiches, butter and jam or Galtee cheese between slices of plain loaf or soda bread; tomatoes and ham were luxuries. We ate these sandwiches around the alley on good days, watchful as hawks in case our places in the queue for games would be taken. On wet days we ate bread and drank milk between the rows of bicycles. The milk was often brought in old medicine bottles corked with rolled newspaper.

Our lunch hours were never supervised. The Brothers had lunch in the big dining-room within the monastery, and afterwards, if the day was dry, they walked up and down the concrete path that ran from the monastery door to the front gate, separated by a lawn and some tall evergreens and one lilac tree from the sanded yard where soccer was played.

For a time, Mr Mannion was the only lay teacher. He taught English, loaned me Dickens from his own library, and was popular both with the Brothers and the boys. He was tall and sandy-haired, came from Galway, had been an army officer, played golf with a half-swing, and drank. On certain days he would return excited from his lunch in town. Then his teaching could be erratic, and was often broken by attempts to kick more heat from the pot-bellied stove in the corner. He wore thick, sponge-soled shoes, and these efforts usually ended with a hurt foot or the smell of burning rubber.

Was the atmosphere of the school religious? Looking back, I do not think it was, certainly not oppressively so. Generally, it was a narrow, restrictive, inward-looking time, dominated by a dark Church that emphasised sin, guilt, death and damnation.

This atmosphere was all about us, like the damp and the wet weather. My feeling is that the wise Brothers thought this sufficient. They did not feel that they had to haul any more low-grade coal from Arigna to the eternal fire. The atmosphere of the school was casual, hard-working, cheerful, even worldly in so far as our low horizons could be said to be of the world. I liked Latin and grew fond of Horace, and when I attempted to smuggle some of his thought into my Irish essay, *Tuairim Pagánta* was written boldly in the margin in red ink, but more in a spirit of mockery or humour than correction. What was marked ruthlessly were grammatical and spelling errors.

Their attitude to what happened outside the classroom was similarly broad-minded and practical. I remember being badly beaten in a fight. Brother Placid would not hear of right or wrong, cause or effect. He ordered my opponent to take me to the hospital to have the wound stitched. As we trudged up the street to the hospital we began to feel like a married couple having to face out to Sunday Mass after a Saturday night shindig, our stupidity growing more painful than any wound with every knowing smile we had to pass.

Brother Damien was very keen that we – or anybody else – should never confuse the Presentation with the Christian Brothers. 'My dear boys', he used to tell us as we prepared to scatter for the summer holidays, 'you will meet people who will assume, once they hear you are attending the Brothers, that *we* are the Christian Brothers. Now, enlighten these people on my behalf that you are *not* attending the Christian Brothers, and that you may be Christian in the sense that you are not pagan, but in no other sense.'

Gradually, the school began to take scholarships and prized examination places away from the diocesan colleges. In my fourth year a second visit from the Brothers found my father and myself again in the potato field. This time it was October and we were digging and pitting the potatoes, and the visitor was Brother Placid, who had replaced Brother Damien as school principal. I had done well that summer in the Intermediate. Brother Placid had been checking the attendances and found that my record in the three years up to the Intermediate was poor. Most of the absences were at regular intervals: a few weeks for potato picking, a week or two around planting time, another two weeks in late April for the turfcutting. Brother Placid took my father to one side, but not out of hearing. He said I was one of his best students and could go far, but not if I was kept from school for several weeks on the way into the Leaving. They walked away together to where Brother Placid had left his bicycle out on the road and stood talking there for some time. My father was silent when he returned to the row of ridges. We worked on until the light began to fail.

As we were covering the new part of the pit with rushes, my father spoke as if he had given lengthy consideration to what he had to say. 'It seems the Brothers think they may be able to make something out of you if you're prepared to work. You better get yourself ready this evening to go to school tomorrow.' When I appeared in school the next morning. Brother Placid just grinned behind the spectacles he was so fond of removing to polish with a white handkerchief. He too was silent.

At a time when corporal punishment was widespread in the home and school, there was little in Carrick-on-Shannon. The personalities of Brothers Placid and Damien contributed to this lack, as well as the fact that there was little need. Almost everybody in the school realized that they were privileged to be getting a secondary education and were anxious to make all the use of it they could. We knew the trains were full of people heading for the night boat and building sites in Britain.

I look back on those five years as the beginning of an adventure that has not stopped. Each day I cycled towards Carrick was an anticipation of delights. The fear and drudgery of school disappeared: without realizing it, through the pleasures of the mind, I was beginning to know and to love the world. The Brothers took me in, set me down, and gave me tools. I look back on my time there with nothing but gratitude, as years of luck and privilege, and, above all, of grace, actual grace.

STRIPED INK
Greg Delanty

I'm smack-dab in the old tabula rasa days, bamboozled
    by the books
    adults bow over, wondering if their eyes light upon
    the white or black spaces,
thinking if only I could read like them I'd understand
    the whole story.
*

A boyhood later, still wren-small, on the top
    storey of The Eagle Printing Company,
witnessing books conjured I think that if I fish in
    them
I'll catch the salmon of knowledge we read
    about at school
out of the river of words and like Fionn I'll
    taste
my burning hand and abracadabra I'll fathom
    hook, line and sinker.
*

But if I'm burnt, it's later that day, my first day as
    floor boy,
when bored of fixing leads, the spirits Fred and
    Dommy working on a new book, dispatch
me down to Christy Coughlan on the box floor
    for a tin of striped ink.
*

The floors of labouring women and men flit by, drowned
    out by the machine's hullabaloo,
framed in the lift's mesh of X's. Somehow between
    floors the elevator conks out
and I'm stuck on my message that I still haven't
    cottoned on to.

MEN WHO ENRICHED MY LIFE

Liam Nolan

In a lifetime of writing I have only ever written at any length about two clergyman. One was an amazing Japanese Lutheran pastor whose name was Kiyoshi Watanabe. He was known among Hong Kong prisoners of war as 'Uncle John', and I wrote a book about him thirty years ago. It was called *Small Man of Nanataki*.

I was so impressed by him and by what he had done in the face of terror and threat, that I wrote to Cardinal Heenan (we lived in England then) and asked him if there was anything disloyal to the Catholic religion in my saying that Watanabe was the greatest Christian I had ever met and that I thought he was a living saint.

How naive we were then! Cardinal Heenan wrote back to me: it was a gentle note of reassurance saying that, having read the book, he probably would have said much the same if *he* had met 'Uncle John'. Cardinal Heenan and Kiyoshi Watanabe are long since dead.

By coincidence, when I received the invitation to write this piece, I had just finished writing my second book about a clergyman, this time a Catholic priest, a Jesuit. His name is Father Diarmuid Ó Peicín. Around the time that the book containing this article is published, my book about Father Ó Peicín, *The Sea Is So Wide*, should also be in the bookshops.

So, here's my third piece prompted by a man of the cloth or, to be accurate, by *men* of the cloth.

I must admit immediately that neither at St Joseph's National School in Cobh, nor at Presentation College, Cobh, was I ever aware of Edmund Rice's existence, let alone his founding of both the Presentation and Christian Brothers.

I'm not sure that the word 'neglected' was entirely appropriate when the Reverend Editor, in his letter of invitation to write for this book, said: 'It could well be that his [the past student's] teachers neglected to mention that Edmund was associated with the school...'.

I don't honestly think that the men who looked after our early educational needs *deliberately* ignored or disregarded Edmund's extraordinary legacy. What they *did* do was pass on to us the fruits of Rice's legacy. They gave us the gift of education.

Over the years, particularly since the practice of re-writing the past became the vogue, I have sometimes mischievously wondered whether the happiness, ordinariness and absence of brutal violence during my school days were figments of my imagination, chimeras, fanciful imaginings induced by brain-washing and subliminal suggestions.

Of course the notion is preposterous. But if that element of our society which insists on the validity of those accounts of cruelty which they continue to parade as memory are entitled to their say, so, too, are people like myself for whom education by the Brothers was an intellectually enriching and pupil-friendly experience.

At Mass in Merrion recently I thought I recognised the man seated to my wife's left. He was small in stature, thin, bordering on the frail, and had wispy white hair. He was deeply immersed in the Mass leaflet, and it was only when the celebrant said: 'Let us now offer each other the sign of peace', that I became certain of his identity.

An old man now, he had been part of my life, and part of my family's life, when he was raven-haired and younger, a Presentation Brother named Kevin. It is a cliché to say that the years rolled back. But they did. Or, rather, that curious mental fast-rewind facility with which we are equipped came into instant action, and I was somehow seeing him standing with my father outside our house on Bellevue Terrace, looking out over the harbour on a summer evening when even the gulls were languid and indifferent. Two small men together, talking and listening to each other with intelligence and respect and, yes, affection.

And then I saw him in Fourth Year and Fifth Year, his head held slightly upwards and sideways, like an alert small bird. He was full of love for language and linguistic beauty, spoke with deep passion about it, and, somehow magically, passed it on. He was enraptured by the magic of words. There is an old saying which I will make bold to change slightly to suit my purpose here: 'There are none so deaf as those who will not hear.'

I listened, I heard, and I have been grateful all my life.

We waited for him when Mass was over. He said that his sight wasn't the best now, that he hadn't been sure whether or not he had recognised me at the moment when we both said: "Peace be with you."

He didn't remain a Presentation Brother always, but, in his heart, he never left the finer things that the Brothers stood for, nor did they leave him.

He brought his wonderful intelligence and his compassion and his teaching gifts to generations of students in Dublin and, as a lay teacher, taught them as he had taught us. They were privileged, as we also had been.

To me he will always be Brother Kevin, though I know his name to be Michael Courtney. I also know from his wife, Sheila, that all of us who were taught by him so many years ago, are still his 'Cobh boys'.

When we were leaving his home that morning after Mass, as he walked with Oonagh towards our car, I said to Sheila, 'I wonder if he has the slightest idea of the immensity of the contribution he made to our lives? Or how much he is cherished by us? Please tell him that I said this – and that I said thanks.'

'He'll be very pleased,' Sheila said. 'He's very proud of his "Cobh boys". He says that his years in Cobh were the happiest years of the whole of his life.'

That gave me quite a lump in my throat. And I hope Brother Kevin/Michael Courtney gets to read these words. Edmund Rice would have been proud of him.

Kevin wasn't the only one from my student days that Edmund Rice would have been proud of.

The chances are that I might never have come across 'The Shooting of Dan McGrew', or any of the other work of that remarkable English-born Canadian poet, Robert William Service, if a Presentation Brother, whose name in religion was Eugenius, hadn't walked into Seventh Class one day after lunch, sat himself on the edge of a table, opened a slim book with a crimson cover, and read in a transatlantic accent:

> A bunch of the boys were whooping it up in the Malamute
> saloon;
> The kid that handles the music-box was hitting a jag-time
> tune;
> Back of the bar, in a solo game, sat Dangerous Dan
> McGrew,
> And watching his luck was his light-o'-love, the lady that's
> known as Lou.

Eugenius, his bald pate shining, his spectacles glinting as his head moved with the turning of each page, read on without looking up, until he came to the very last words of the poem, which are the same as the last words of the first verse – 'the lady that's known as Lou.'

The only sound in that classroom at the end was the sound of exhaled breath.

He held the book up. I read the black lettering on the red cover. There were just two lines. The first said: *SONGS OF A SOURDOUGH.* The second line said: Robert W. Service.

I've never forgotten that day – Eugenius saying, 'Now, men, what do you think of that?' and, without waiting for an answer, adding, 'Robert Service!', while shaking his head in wonder at the lines he had read.

'Nux' McCormack, alongside me in the front row, said, 'Fantastic!'. I think I said, 'That's amazing altogether!'

Eugenius flicked through the pages until he found what he was looking for, cleared his throat, and said, 'Now, listen to this:'

> I wanted the gold, and I sought it;
> I scrabbled and mucked like a slave.
> Was it famine or scurvy – I fought it,
> I hurled my youth into the grave.

This time, in the course of his reading, he occasionally let his eyes stray from the page to look up and out of the window to somewhere very far away as he spoke lines like:

> The strong life that never knows harness;

The wilds where the caribou call;
The freshness, the freedom, the farness –
O God! How I'm stuck on it all.

The man was a romantic – and Principal of the 'Nash' (as the Presentation Brothers' National School was known) at the same time.

During the ten-minute morning break at eleven o'clock, and again before lunch hour ended at 1.30 p.m., he would walk smartly backwards and forwards along the raised portion of the yard immediately in front of the statue of St Joseph. He was usually in the company of 'Spud' Murphy, or Liam O'Sullivan, or Tom Cooney, or all three.

I can still see that characteristic pigeon-toed walk of his, his eyes invariably looking at the grey, cracking cement at his feet, his forehead furrowed in concentration. I often wondered what they spoke about – the 'freshness, the freedom, the farness'? Or something much more mundane, like neutrality or ration books, or the Cobh Charitable Coal Fund, which had no coal at all but a shed full of crumbling turf for 'the poor'?

Other Brothers – Prudent (small, round-faced, dark), Raphael (tall, white-haired, insubstantial), Cormac (reddish-haired, burly, looking as if there was a temper lurking below the surface), Linus (lean and lethal-looking) – formed their own black-garbed groups, the numbers carefully chosen so that there would be no need to sidestep as they passed each other on the walking area.

We waited for the moment when Eugenius would break away, raise his referee's whistle to his lips, and with cheeks bulging like Louis Armstrong's, blow a piercing blast for the small universe of the schoolyard to freeze into immobility.

In the classroom he could be as stern-faced as was necessary, but, if you looked closely, you could always detect the tell-tale signs of an ill-hidden smile. He was so human! He had enthusiasm and a sense of humour, and, at appropriate moments, treated us as if we were adults. It was a glorious and never-abused compliment.

Eugenius loved to swim, and like another Brother (Regis), who would come into the lives of those of us who went on to

Presentation College, he loved to look at the world in which we lived – and I mean look, really look, whether it was at our brown and withered winters, or at the flaming grandeur of red sunsets.

These men of the Presentation Brothers marked our lives for the better. And when you caught glimpses of them walking among the apples trees, silent and in prayer, you were seeing spirituality at its most private and precious. They never, in my experience, tried to hammer sanctity into us. Theirs *was* a personal holiness, and, in the area of religion, it *was* by their example that they influenced. Yes, Edmund Rice would have been proud of them, as I am now.

Gentlemen, I thank you!

NO REGRETS, NO CHIPS, JUST THANKS

Alan Titley

I have always thought autobiography to be the first refuge of the writer bereft of imagination and the last refuge of the person with nothing to say. Certainly, experience of Irish literature this century has given us rich and thick examples out of the memoir industry of everything from the dull and plodding to the sloppy and slushy. Writing about self has been variously drawn from a past that was so beautiful that it never could have existed, even while going through the fields to school, or so awful that it would have taken a dark and barracked sensibility to invent. Most of us have lived with a mottled experience that we have never presumed to have been so different from anybody else's that we feel it should be thrust upon the public, either as self-congratulation or self-flagellation – with their attendant pleasures for the writer.

Besides, memory is the most porous and fleeting of sieves. We all come through because of a birdy-song practice of memory – a little bit of this and a little bit of that. But why those little bits survive rather than the long days and weeks and months that vanish forever is something that the greatest committees of psychologists and and brain surgeons will never answer. We remember neither birth nor death and most of life in between is an erased tablet. Yet what we still do every day is a result of what we have learned, and more particularly of what we have learned so well that we cannot recall when we first knew it.

Like everyone else I can vividly remember my first day at school, or, if I can't I have invented it from numerous essays which I must have been forced to write. But I do not remember my second day, or my third, or my seventh, or my three thousand and thirty-third. And yet they must have been the days in which the learning was done, in which the forgotten bits were put together to help me know what I think I now know. For schooling is a matter of routine rather than a series of eurekas and epiphanies, a matter of slowly acquired skills rather than the miraculous opening of doors and windows upon enchanting vistas.

So my only contribution to autobiography has to be the grateful acknowledgement of all that I have forgotten I ever learned but which I now demonstrably know. There are, of course, the anecdotes of this teacher or that who by force of personality or by the good fortune of eccentricity has given us stories to tell round the fire or in the club or wherever takes your fancy when sentimentality calls. And there are those moments of illumination which come by accident or good fortune when all the groundwork has been done. But teaching, no less than learning, is primarily a matter of slog and slog again, which is not in any way an excuse for it to be boring, but a recognition that the first business of a school is to impart skills and knowledge and that all other things shall be added thereto.

I had the fortune and grace to be blessed with good teachers and good teaching almost all of my instructed life both in Scoil Chríost Rí national school and later in Coláiste Chríost Rí secondary school. I knew they were good because there were always those few who did not measure up and we all knew the difference. You might say, 'So what? Teachers are supposed to be good no more or no less than any other professional.' I have no stick to measure the competence of teachers against doctors or dockers or consultants or coopers, but during a life spent in education at first, second and third levels and in three continents, both giving and receiving, I have no doubt that what I got from school was of the highest standard and for me something very special. There are no chips on the shoulders and no gripes in the belly. Being grateful is not as strong or as grabbing a feeling as blaming it all on one's roots or on some teacher or on an 'irrelevant' curriculum, but it is the seedbed from which we all grow.

Nothing too exciting yet: no beatings, no abuse, no savagery, no narrow-minded jingoistic Jansenism. As a writer I have been cursed with a happy childhood and a fulfilling education. More pain and bigotry might have led to a livelier appreciation of the autowritings of the begrudgers. This is not to deny the toughness of it for those for whom it was tough, but we have lived enough in the world to differentiate between the bitter harshness of reality and the literary expectations of fashion. Education itself should begin to be a bulwark against disappointment and the false consciousness of being always sinned against.

In the debate between free will and determinism we have no choice but to plump for the former. And yet if asked what is the single greatest determining factor in anyone's life I am tempted to say it is luck. Fate is an older word, grace a Christian one. Strip the wrapping from luck, however, and you get a convergence of personal, social and historical factors which can at least be partly explained.

Luck in education does not and did not fall unbidden from the sky. It comes about because someone, somewhere, decided to do something, somehow. The education that the Presentation Brothers give and have given has come about because Edmund Rice decided that it should be so. It could have been otherwise. It could have been that it never was. That he did was grace, or fortune, or luck, but it can never be said that it was not good, nor great, nor for the betterment of many generations of Irish children.

Down the line in Coláiste Chríost Rí of the 1960s the glow of that decision to educate the everybodies was still warm.

Sometimes when I hear the word 'ethos' I want to go for my gunge-detector. It is certainly an over-used and now much shrivelled word that is desperately trying to capture the ineffable and intangible. Ethos can most certainly not be bottled or packaged or marketed or nailed to the ground. And when you read certain English public-school memoirs overflowing with ethos you wish the Greeks had never had a word for it. It may, however, be just a fancy word for 'atmosphere'or, to be more accurate, atmosphere with a purpose attached. And we can never deny that places and events and times and people have atmosphere, whatever else they lack.

The problem is in detaching or unpacking the specifics of the school from the specifics of time and place and personality. No doubt it cannot be done. I do recall us being inordinately and unjustifiably confident whether we were taking part in games or debates or drama festivals. The fact that we were often beaten didn't dent that confidence. I was later told that this is just part of the Cork swagger which can never admit to being second best to anyone despite much evidence of the senses. But I never remember anyone telling us we were better than everyone else. Was this just a raw and callow youth imbued with the brash indomitability of the sixties? Or a false shining face to hide the pimply doubts?

I rather think that the special atmosphere of Coláiste Chríost Rí had its origins in much more specific places. I have already said that the first and main purpose of a school is to teach the curriculum and to do so as well as it possibly can. No fudging on this. Gallons of ethos awash in the corridors of a school cannot compensate for bad or lazy teaching. All the galas and fêtes and horsey days and fancy gee-gaws that are tacked on to a school are totally worthless if the teaching ain't done.

The trick is this and somebody in Coláiste Chríost Rí (at least) copped on to it without turning it into a philosophy that could be explicitly pronounced and then killed. It must have been an instinct, a sense of just what is right beyond book, bell or candle. Good teaching is an art, and art springs from instinct, and instinct is a gift of the spirit. The trick is this: extra-curricular activities are not *extra,* they are of the pith and gut and marrow. Or to put it another way: you cannot teach the curriculum by just teaching the curriculum, and if you try to do so you will surely fail. The waters of knowledge do not course between well-constructed banks, they seep and leak and overflow and fertilise all around them just as they receive fresh streams and globs of sludge from wherever they must.

Without reaching for my photograph album I remember operas, musicals, full-length plays, one-act plays, debates, public speaking, question-times, choirs – all, it should be said, in both Irish and English – as part of the natural world. This may not have been a great deal unusual as it is probable that many other schools did likewise, although I do think that the *extent* to which students participated in these was extraordinary. More unusual however, may have been the existence of, for example, a music society where students came and played and discussed their favourite music. And it didn't matter whether this was classical, or folk, or blues, or jazz, or traditional, or rock.

The world and *The Cork Examiner* told us that our teachers frowned on all this pop culture and here they were encouraging us to talk about it! Music could be discussed and argued over and haggled about just like a subject on the course. And, hang on, there was a film society. It is only in the last few years that the major art form of the twentieth century has begun to crawl apologetically into university courses, and here we were being persuaded by a few enlightened teachers that *The Magnificent Seven* wasn't just another cowboy and Indian bang-bang.

They will say now that we didn't have the 'vocabulary' – meaning jargon – to deal with it, but some kind of education begins when you see your teachers recognising magic.

Of course, Gilbert and Sullivan and silent movies and Buddy Holly didn't have anything directly to do with the curriculum and parents who thought that their sons' time was being wasted might have had cause for complaint (they wouldn't really) if all this was being done during school hours. It wasn't. Most teachers gave of their free time in something. We never supposed this to be unusual. I know now that it is.

But hang on just another minute. We had a genius of an English teacher, Mr Fehilly, who insisted that we read the newspapers. To ensure that we did this he brought us in articles from *The Observer's* international news service once a week. This was time taken, stolen and cadged from the precious allotment to the curriculum. Parents then were just as conscious of honours grades as they are now of the dreaded points. To my knowledge they didn't baulk. I do recall one narrowly-focused swot suggesting that this was a waste of time but he was descended upon by the rest of the class and unceremoniously gagged. There seems to have been an inherent understanding that to know any one thing well you had to know a lot else besides and that the curriculum was only a guide to knowledge. How can you deal with history, literature, geography or commerce without knowing about the world? How can any education be false if it introduces you to all the ways of the world and the pathways through it?

And we had an Irish teacher, Roibeárd Ó hÚrdail, who realised that in order to know the language you had to know the culture and the culture was all around us. We had, each and everyone, presumed that all the good poets were dead poets because they were the only ones on the course; he introduced us to the living poets *who were not on the curriculum* and in *our Leaving Cert year* by teaching us poems by Seán Ó Ríordáin (then unknown to the Department of Education) and by informing us that he walked the streets of Cork alive and well and might be met with in Liam Ruiséal's bookshop on a Saturday afternoon. The thought that a real, modern, unhistorical poet resided and inhered in Cork shivered our timbers and boggled more than our minds. Roibeárd Ó hÚrdail also taught us songs not on the course when we could have been grappling with yet another grammatical ploy. An insistence on high standards is often seen as shorthand for demanding tight, accurate, correct, precise and unimaginative work. The high standards I was taught rose up because they expanded to include the world and the then present day. In the stupidest of phrases 'it was relevant', even though I full well realise that relevance is something we must all make for ourselves.

The usual dull souls of educational theory make much nowadays of integrated curriculums and interdisciplinary studies. There is nothing new here. Good teachers in all times and in every place make educational connections because they are there. The universe in the grain of sand is still an apt image. But it has always puzzled me why our own education in Coláiste Chríost Rí was so *liberal* (a word I hesitate to use because of its since-accreted connotations). In the folklore of modern Ireland an education by 'the Brothers' was supposed to be synonymous with bigotry and narrow-mindedness and paranoia. It was meant to be closed and final and definitive and even propagandistic. Experience has taught me that this has always been a parody and parody is often the bile of honour.

No more than ethos, to talk of a Christian education nowadays can invite a quiver in the pen and a shiver in the spine and a question-mark hovering over the brain. This is because Christianity is an ideal and any attempt to realise it falls short. The hole, therefore, between rhetoric and reality gapes wide. Ideology can never meet the world on the level of quotidian ordinary experience. In the battle between living and theory, living wins hands down, every time. Yet living is lived and guided because of somebodies someplaces giving us directions.

Edmund Rice was inspired by the Christian vision but in the

most practical of ways. People, young people, should know about life in their time and place and this should be informed by the spirit of Christianity, that is to say, of Christ. This is, again, where a non-preacher in the obvious Christian way begins to have doubts. To use the words of Christianity at all invites rejection. But somebody or somebodies in Coláiste Chríost Rí in the 1960s, consciously or otherwise realised, no more than the educational curriculum, that Christianity belonged to the real world of here and now and us. Any idea of life must be involved in life and inhering in it.

Christ went around telling stories; we dealt with literature. Christ went around doing things; we were taught the skills of the world. Christ led by example; I like to think that we also were led by example. Christianity lives in art, in science, in commerce, in getting things done, in dealing with it, in fulfilling your talents. The bark of the dogma gives a poor response compared with the bite of being there and doing that.

Religion is not a matter of statues, plastic or plaster, moving or bleeding, with all the attendant kitsch. Religion in Ireland never had the advantage of being pared down to the non-prescriptive do-goodery of apologetic Protestantism, or the over-indulgent and gloriously excessive wonder of Eastern Orthodox Catholicism. It has touched on these, of course, and wavered hither and thither. Its strength has been its direct involvement in everyday life, an involvement which has always resulted in a healthy balance between proper respect for the clergy and a wariness where they might overstep their bounds. But these bounds were always broadly drawn because of this involvement. Christianity has always been central to education in Ireland because to know is to wonder, to know a little is to want more, to know at all is an extension of the soul.

A pedestal is no place for a teacher, lay or brother or priest or nun, to be. Wonder and longing and a thirst for justice come from below. All imagination is moral imagination ultimately. Education must dirty its hands with the mire of the everyday and shoot for the stars of the good and the true. There are no frontiers except those made by inadequate understanding. I think I got this from my teachers and I like to think I still have it.

Because if I don't they have certainly failed.

The reason autobiography is a tired medium for tired minds is because there is still, and always, so much more to be done. Just as solemnity is the homage we pay to the mundane, a memoir is a monument to the spiritually dead. All we can do is acknowledge our gratitude and move on.

THE WALL
Patrick Galvin

The wall stood
In the village square
And no one knew
Who put it there or why.
It served no purpose
It belonged to no one
And it was built a mile away
From the sea.

You could measure our days
By the wall.

When a man died
We placed a stone on the wall
When a woman died
We placed two stones on the wall
And when a child died
We placed a small pebble on the wall
And you could feel
The bleeding.

You could measure our griefs
By the wall.

Sometimes,
We drew faces on the wall.
We carved our names on the wall
We drew small boats
Large fish
And storms at sea –
And one man painted
A lighthouse.

You could measure our lights
By the wall.

And
If you stood close to the wall
You could hear the Earth moving
The stars falling
And the sun sinking
Slowly
Into a fading sea.

You could measure our dark
By the wall.

WHAT PRES MEANT TO ME

Michael J. Kelleher

Most people remember their first day at school. I don't. I do remember however an autumn day when my father told me that I would soon be going to school. I did not like the sound of it at all. My brother Humphrey had been there for three years and, in my childhood view, was no better for the experience. My younger sister, Gretchen, had a different attitude. She could not wait to get there and had already acquired a satchel.

I knew that my childhood freedom would be trammelled in some way that would limit my well-stocked imagination. I was right. When the day came, I went without demur. Not so my best friend, David. He held out for almost three weeks. Eventually, parental pressure won.

I was sitting in class near the old school yard and next to the county library when I heard the hullabaloo. David and his father were hardly past St Joseph's school on the Mardyke when his resistance increased to violent opposition. Eventually the door of the classroom was thrown open and David Junior, valiant to the last, rushed across the room and kicked Brother Innocent in the shins. His courage, I thought, was commendable. Eventually, a truce was hammered out and David was put sitting next to me.

Soon we were in competition for different reasons. I could manage mental arithmetic pretty well and even learned the alphabet. However, written symbols were beyond me. This deficit, which went unrecognised by both my parents and the school, probably altered my perspective on life. I was almost into secondary school before I learned to read. Under the modern secondary school entrance examination system I probably wouldn't have made it. Hence, I am glad that such arrangements did not apply when I was a boy.

In fact, I won the competition with David. He came second last in the class but I beat him by achieving the lowest grade. As the years tumbled by, the situation got worse. My natural ability at maths was no advantage if I could not read the questions. Once, in Fifth Class, Brother Alban presented us with a particularly difficult problem. Each boy was asked to read the question first and then suggest how it might be done. Each read without difficulty but none could give the answer. When it came to my turn, the Brother said there was no point in asking me. He was incorrect, however. I had surmised what the problem was and, because I knew, I was able to state how it could be tackled. He was genuine, if surprised, in his praise.

Brother Alban died last year. He looked in ill-health even then but, nonetheless, lived to a great age. One other issue arose during that year which imprinted itself upon my mind and his. It had to do with confirmation. Someone asked how it was that souls who went to Purgatory a thousand years ago had to wait a longer time for the last day. No one could offer an explanation. I suggested, however, that there was no such thing as time in a purely spiritual world.

Today we are all regrettably familiar with our children having to get grinds so that they attain the desired level of points in the Leaving Cert examination. I must have been one of the few who had to get a grind for his Confirmation because of my inability to read. Another boy, Gerard, was given the task of teaching me the written questions and answers. No one recognised what my real problem was.

I have an association with Pres that goes back over fifty years. I was at no other school. My three brothers also attended, as did my four sons. The next generation has not yet arrived but, when they do, I hope the association with my old school will continue.

We Pres boys of the 1940s and 1950s knew little of Edmund Rice. The Brothers had told us about him but we assumed he had founded the Christian rather than the Presentation Brothers. And the latter were our rivals on the rugby field. Brother Innocent, who, by this time, had been to university and was now our science teacher, told us that the two groups of Brothers had fallen out over food! The official view, given us by Brother De Sales, was that it was about spiritual authority. In those days and in our minds, however, Edmund Rice, although the inspiration of both, was primarily the spiritual property of the 'other' college.

Edmund Rice was a remarkable man. It is fitting that he is to be beatified this year. He represents all that is good in education. It is right, and has so been regarded since ancient classical times, that the older should service the younger. An ancient Indian proverb says that 'as the calf loves to suckle, so also does the cow love to give suck'. So it is in education, whether given by a loving parent or a dedicated teacher. Edmund Rice was both. He served the young with his mighty mind.

Many Irish men in this century, as well as the last one, have been in debt to the Brothers, whether Christian or Presentation. Thousands, like me, received an excellent education, either totally free or for virtually nothing, in money terms. There must, however, be concern for the future. What will happen if, and when, the Brothers are gone?

The charisma of Edmund Rice pervades the Brothers' schools. In Pres, in my time, all of the teachers in the primary school were Brothers. This differed from the secondary where the majority were lay teachers. The same spirit, however, obtained. They were all family men (no women teachers in those days!). When we sat our examinations and tests, they waited outside to see how we got on. There was no question of short-changing the student. The teacher was like a good football coach committed to his team.

Regrettably, today, some of our schools may have changed. Grinds, not only for the slow or backward, seem to be on the way to becoming a big business. Some teachers may even work harder outside of school time than they do within. Schoolchildren can thus become grind fodder in an increasingly materialistic age. Intelligence, or what passes for measurements of it, is the new morality. Scientific evidence, however, suggests that it is personality, more then anything else, that determines success in later life. For many the worship of Baal is everything. Other people are not considered.

Puberty and emergent manhood brought other problems for me in secondary school. Football was never an abiding interest of mine. Yet, suddenly, it appeared important to get on the school team. I rightly calculated that the scrum, at least in those days, could hide patent lack of football skills. Pat Barry, the dedicated school coach, was well used to shaping teams out of minimal resources. For him I was no exception. After many back-breaking afternoons a prop forward was created. I was proud.

All was not sunshine, however. A lay teacher know as 'Battle-axe' endeavoured to cut me down to size. For some misdemeanour, long forgotten by me, I heard him roar, 'Come up here, Ceilleachair!' 'Battle-axe' came from the country. He was doing his Higher Dip.Ed. We, city slickers, had often joked about his two suits, one pin-striped brown and one of a similar cloth in blue. Each was worn on alternate weeks. We surmised that his mother had told him they would last longer that way with the added advantage that the unobservant might assume he was the possessor of many such garments.

The use of the 'Ceilleachair' identified him as a country boy. City folk called me 'Kelleher'. When I reached the top of the class, he opened his attaché case and took out a large leather strap. To my curious eye, this was part of the belly band for a horse. 'Bend over, Ceilleachair', he said. This I did and he administered four of his hurling best.

Several things seemed to happen to me all at once. There was shock, pain and a rising heat. There was also a sense of injustice. Worst of all, I vacillated between my concept of myself as an emerging man and my fear that I would cry. In fact, my eyes filled up. Suddenly, almost to my own surprise, I raised my hand to draw the teacher's attention once more. 'What's the matter with you now, Ceilleachair?', he shouted from the top of the class. 'Sir', I said, with all the irony I could muster, 'How much did you get for the horse?'

The class burst out laughing, enjoying the ridicule which they rightly construed as restoring an unequal balance. 'Battle-axe', himself, shared in the laughter. For this I was and am grateful.

Education, after all, is an interaction between two unequal powers. The teacher, who is expected to know more, and to be skilled in educing knowledge out of his charges; and the student, who knows less but ideally has the virtue of freshness and a new way of looking at things. Such a dynamic relationship is never static. And its very liveliness may provoke instability in a changing world.

The good teacher, and for that matter the good school also, is in a sense like a helmsmen. There is a point in the horizon which he intends to reach. To do this, however, he must take wind and tide direction into consideration. By tacking back and forth he makes the desired landfall. In the to and fro between pupil and teacher the future personality of the boy is shaped.

So also the future of the school. I hope Pres remains vibrant in the twenty-first century. I believe that the spirit of Edmund Rice demands that structures be put in place to ensure the continuance of his ideal. Independent schools, in the absence of Brothers, will need a board of governors to whom the headmaster will report. The salary of a head should be commensurate with the board's expectations of his stewardship. Bright boys ought not to need special tuition. If they do, there is something wrong with the system.

Most primary schools in the country are now co-educational, as are all colleges of tertiary education. It is increasingly an anachronism that many secondary schools are still either for boys or girls only. No doubt, this will also change in the years ahead.

Edmund Rice saw a social evil and responded to it by dedicating his own life and wealth to popular education and providing a model which many of his contemporaries felt compelled to follow. If he were alive today, would he see himself as a Presentation or as a Christian Brother? This, however, would be analogous to asking, if St Patrick returned, would he visualise himself as an Irish Catholic or an Irish Protestant? It is likely that both would see the questions as impertinent and irrelevant. Instead, each would use his vision to shape the future of our people. And Edmund Rice would most certainly modify his school structures to accommodate all the intervening social changes.

AILBIE

Jim Cremin

I knocked. My knuckles made little impression on the heavy oak door. I waited and, like a rabbit on the threshold of a new forest, eavesdropping, I hoped no one would answer. It was my first day at school and I was late.

It wasn't really my fault. It was Ted Hackett's. After all he was eight: I was only four and a half. My mother had given him a penny to guarantee my safe conduct from Gillabbey Street, up Warren's Lane, across Bandon Road and up to Greenmount Primary School which topped our hill. At Downey's he slipped in to buy a slab of Cleeves' toffee. There was a week's chewing in it and Ted wasn't going to give up the immediate pleasures of the tacky toffee for any of the promised but distant rewards of education.

Late! My mother, if she knew, would have murdered me. No expense had been spared in preparing me for school. I was kitted out from skull-cap to shoes in Norton's on Lavitt's Quay. In the Coal Quay I had obtained a chequered satchel with straps and buckles, and, from a Thompson's bread van, a pencil and a jotter – for free. I even had a pencil sharpener.

On the way out that morning Mum had also given me a penny, the one with the chicken on it, but had warned me against going on a spending spree. 'Give that to the monks', she said, 'it's for the black babies'.

It was my first experience of reverse racial discrimination. I was a white baby and pennyless. My father had once shown me Africa on an atlas. A hop, step and jump across France and there it was sticking out from the page like a huge elephant's ear. Tarzan and the monks were our only links between Cork and that vast continent where my father had told me the Presentation Brothers, armed only with chalk and blackboards, roamed among fearsome, ring-nosed African tribes.

So I had good reason to fear the monks! Every time I passed

the gates to Greenmount I peered in at that austere Victorian building, at the same time clutching my mother tightly. I felt threatened by the austere exterior of the building with its outside staircase and what looked to me like barred windows. In my young imagination there were three great prisons in the world. My father had told me stories of two, Sing Sing and Alcatraz; the third, Greenmount National School, I could see for myself.

I had often seen the boys marching out to the yard, holding hands, in regimented orderly lines, like a chain gang. There also I had spied the black-robed Brothers, locally called 'monks', walking up and down among the boys, like jailors. And Ted Hackett told me that at the entrance to the 'Dya' field, there were shackles! That very morning he had gone further and confided in a whisper that there was a dungeon behind the hand-ball alley for boys who got their sums wrong. The whole place seemed to me like a gigantic house of correction.

'Some day, you'll be there', my mother had often said, not meaning it as a warning. Now the fateful moment had come: I stood outside the door ready to begin my sentence. To my right a class started up a chorus of ten times tables: the chant was relentless but, apparently, unrehearsed. 'Ten times!', I thought. They must be the 'biggies', perhaps Fourth or Fifth Class. I was a 'smallie' waiting outside the door of the junior infants, then known in the school as the 'Abby Abs'.

The door opened. Above me towered a Falstaffian figure in a black soutane, gathered at the waist with a wide black leather belt. I had only once previously seen a buckle as big as that: it was on the belt worn by the giant in *Jack and the Beanstalk*. What was he going to say? Perhaps something in Latin about the virtues of punctuality. Perhaps a warning not to bother him in the future for a reference. He raised his spectacles on to his forehead and looked down at me.

'And you must be Jim Cremin?', he said.
As he shook it, my cold tiny hand got lost in the geography of his palm, in all its bumps and wrinkled valleys, in the warmth of its climate.

'I was waiting for you. I'm so glad you could make it. Now let me take your coat and bag. I'm Brother Ailbie.'

159

Ailbie confused me no end. 'Now let me show you to your place', he said.

I was expecting a prison, the swish of canes, the yelps of inmates. Instead I was being ushered as if entering some prestigious hotel. From the desk an inkwell looked up at me like a blackened eye. On either side of it, in small grooves, two nibless pens lay waiting. Ailbie placed my bag on the seat and gave it a reassuring pat as if it were a little animal. 'Now that is settled', he said, 'come and join the rest of us.'

The rest were gathered around a fire at the top of a huge classroom. It was like bonfire night. A crescent moon of illuminated faces peered in at the flames as they forked over and under logs only to meet again in a hot embrace of red and yellow knots. Now and then a log would snap like a Christmas cracker. Behind us the desks were empty, the blackboard clean and our jotters asleep for the day in unopened satchels.

The peace was broken by Con Carney (later nicknamed 'Chilli') bawling for his mother.

'Now I have just the thing for you', said Ailbie. His hand dug deep inside his pocket, as if searching in a sack, and from it he produced a tiny, royal blue, empty ink bottle and placed it up and under Connie's eyelid.

'Now you just go ahead and fill that for us'.

Instead of gazing at the fire we all turned and stared at Connie holding the tiny bottle to his eye. His bawl moderated, slid down the scale, became a whimper, then a moan and finally ceased. Later, I was to learn that this was called 'peer pressure'. Later, also, when I began to study to be a teacher myself, and conscientiously read what the psychologists had to say about early childhood education, I discovered that Ailbie had been practising many of the latest theories thirty years earlier.

Only last week I read a piece by somebody suggesting that it would help students in the transition from primary to post-primary school if they were taken on a tour of the new school. I recalled again my first day in Greenmount. Ailbie lined us up. The first boy grasped his soutane, then each boy caught hold of the one in front and off we went for a tour of the entire school. Ailbie himself walked with a prodigal foot that kept veering sideways. Together we were like a kite with many ribbons. We were dressed in a jumbled collection pullovers, jumpers, hand-me-downs. But he led us out the door, along the corridor, in and out of every classroom, up and around rows of desks. Sometimes bullies bared their teeth and assaulted us with a chorus of, 'Abbey Abs, Duncie Dees, forty years at ABC'.

But they had no effect on us. We knew we had Ailbie.

How I wish I could recall the conversation around the fire that morning but, unfortunately, I can't. But I can certainly recall the loud knock on the door about ten o'clock, more like a kick than a knock. Ailbie said in what was then a strange language, which could easily have been African, 'A Shéamaisín! Oscail an doras, má's é do thoil', at the same time pointing at the door.

Divining his meaning in some strange way, I opened the door, though not without trepidation. A woman I later came to know as Katie Keane entered with a huge pot of steaming cocoa. The room filled with the odour of chocolate and our noses responded. She also delivered a tray of plastic mugs and a banquet of buns. These buns were so large that they had to be embraced with both hands. Down the sides of each bun slid an avalanche of fresh icing. Silent heads bowed as we dug down into these buns, down into the cocoa, coming up now and then to gaze at our new surroundings. The silence was broken only by burps, the crackling of the fire and the odd belch. This was true education as far as I was concerned. This was progress. A four-and-a-half-year-old from a tenement room above a shop in Gillabbey Street and already I was dining out. And when it was all gone what sweet goodbyes it left on my fingers and about my lips!

So there we were on a Monday morning around our fire. There were different worlds outside the security of those windows. North Korea was invading its neighbour down south, the USSR was trying to keep up with the US of A. Even in Cork, I already saw people who were economically worlds apart from me. But here was a child's first day at school as it should be. The reality of the universal brotherhood of man was being acted out with hot chocolate and iced buns around a roaring fire. It was the world according to Ailbie.

In my own class in school some weeks ago we were reading the

Gospel according to John. A student had asked me what was the last thing Jesus did on earth. I flicked through *The Living Bible* and found the answer on page nine hundred and twenty-two. For those of you as unfamiliar with the Bible as myself, I should say the chapter relates the story of the apostles fishing in Lake Galilee on a damp day and, not untypically, catching nothing. Coming ashore frustrated and wet they were met by the risen Jesus. He had a fire lighting, fish frying, some brew and some bread.

It is reassuring to note that the last thing Jesus did on earth was simply to provide food and warmth for those to whom he had committed his life.

It was the first thing Ailbie did. He had a sound knowledge of children, education and the message of Jesus.

DUISKE
William Wall

This abbey of Duiske raised again
    the year of our lord 1980
    not a nail in its roof
of unseasoned oak, not a stone
unturned for His praise. Let the wind

blow now, let old miseries batter
    as always and new
    afflictions bring us low –
His house has a safe roof;
in Duiske his head is dry.

IMPRESSIONS OF PRES

John Fraher

The first decision I had to make when I started in Pres was whether or not to play rugby. This was the only area where there was serious pressure to conform. I decided not to be dragooned, because sport seemed to me to be essentially unimportant, and there were many more interesting and fulfilling things to do. One self-defining boundary had been drawn, somewhat painfully, since it marked one off from most of the class as part of an odd minority with values which were difficult to understand.

Unexpectedly, the religious side of things wasn't emphasised anything like as much as rugby. Religion, mostly Catholic of course, was presented for understanding and discussion, but without emotive pressure to conform one way or another. Of course, the hope was that you would see the Catholic way, but it was left very much to yourself to decide. There were no disagreeable Jesuitical attempts at moulding minds. Arguments and points of view were presented in a fair-minded and balanced way, not without humour. This whole approach made a very strong impression. It reflected the general easy atmosphere generated by the teachers, which fostered tolerance and freedom of choice, within reasonable limits of course. This approached contrasted strongly with the intolerance and oppressive conformity of 1950s Irish society. It offered a means of bypassing this and working out one's own priorities.

Pragmatism characterised the approach to teaching. The school was there to teach, to enable one to do as well as possible in exams, on the basis that this offered the best possible opportunity to fulfil your potential afterwards, if that was what you wanted. There was no extreme pressure; how hard you worked was left up to yourself within reason. That approach was very effective within the constraints of the secondary school system of the time, in helping each individual to succeed as well as possible. Essentially, you got on with learning and there wasn't much nonsense about creating an artificial ethos within which the school was perceived as some kind of organism which moulded your thinking and development in conformity with a defined stereotype. Outside the strict boundaries of teaching, the largely unspoken implication was that you were free to choose how to develop yourself as an individual within a framework of social responsibility and decency.

The pragmatic focus on teaching for exam results went too far in that it emphasised maths and science subjects because the highest scores could be obtained in these. The division between C.P. Snow's Two Cultures was very much in evidence, with the sciences pre-eminent. Apart from the ideologically-driven dominance of Irish, which was universal in all schools, the absence of a modern language from the curriculum was particularly unfortunate. Latin was taught, and still should be, because of the rigour and discipline which it instils. However, the secondary status of subjects like history resulted in gaps in knowledge, and greatly reduced awareness of the importance of the humanities in both personal and cultural terms. Paradoxically, trying to fill these gaps has given me enormous pleasure ever since.

A PRESENTATION JOURNEY

Pat Coffey

The last number of years has witnessed a resurgence of interest in the life and work of Edmund Ignatius Rice. In this, the year of his beatification, this interest has quickened and come into particular focus. The two congregations of which he is founder, the Presentation Brothers and the Christian Brothers, have each embodied his charism and spirit in their own unique fashions and these traditions have been mediated and developed by generations of Brothers over the decades. The Presentation expression of Edmund's spirit is the one which I personally encountered since a very early stage in my life. In the course of these pages I would like to recall just a number of experiences, incidents and insights which revealed to me this particular expression of Edmund's charism.

I was born in the Lough Parish in Cork, literally within a stone's throw of Greenmount National School, known affectionately to the locals at that time as 'The Green'. The limestone and old red sandstone of Greenmount National School, built by the Presentation Brothers in 1854, together with the Lough Chapel and St Finbarr's Cathedral dominated the landscape of my childhood and I first saw the light of day in the centre of a triangle formed by them. Going to the 'Green' was as natural for me as breathing air. My father, my uncles and my own brother had been there before me and my father had always spoken affectionately and respectfully about individual Presentation Brothers who had taught him. Their names elude me right now but his positive attitude towards them remains clearly etched on my consciousness. I also have happy memories of my own schooling and these too have remained with me over the years.

Greenmount School was, indeed, a happy place to be. It did, of course, hold moments of minor terror. These were the normal fears experienced by all schoolboys at the time in relation to lessons not fully learned or understood and the consequences which resulted from this. My abiding impression of my teachers, however, and with one exception they were all Brothers, was of men who were extremely hard-working, happy in their teaching and fair in their treatment of the boys in their charge. A smile came more readily to their faces than a frown as they watched us charge and stampede like wild buffalo around the school yard and the adjoining playing field. Because of its associations with 'The Barrs', being an important nursery to that most illustrious of hurling clubs, Greenmount is, perhaps, best remembered by most of its past pupils in sporting terms. My memories of it, however, have more to do with music. I can still hear the strains of the Greenmount Industrial School Band, then Cork's equivalent of the Artane Boys Band, as it marched proudly up Green Street in its black and red uniform, wheeled through the imposing gates at its southern end and onto the long avenue which led back to 'The Indus.'. I also have memories of conducting the senior infants' percussion band as it cacophonously entertained proud parents in the Fr O'Leary Hall on Bandon Road. In the years that followed I played tin whistle and drums in the school flageolet band, took my first steps in Irish dancing on the road to becoming the Michael Flatley of Greenmount, participated enthusiastically in the school operettas and, with scores of others from the 'Green', sang in the Lough Church choir.

On reflection it seems to me that this veritable explosion of rhythm and harmony had a significant influence, not only on my own personal growth and education in the broadest sense, but also in turning me towards the Brothers. As evidence of this I can cite a particular incident. In my final year in primary school a number of boys in sixth class, myself included, were invited to sing at the Brothers' Christmas morning Mass in the chapel of what had been the Industrial School but which was now the new Presentation Brothers Juniorate of Coláiste Therese. I recall vividly the fear I experienced as I nervously walked alone up that long dark avenue at what seemed an unearthly hour of the morning. I also remember, however, the warm welcome and good-humoured, lavish generosity which we experienced in appreciation of our efforts. This, for some reason or other, made a lasting impression on me. At that moment I didn't know that within less than a year I would make my way back up that avenue, complete with cardboard suitcase, to spend three years in the Juniorate.

In ways the transfer from Greenmount National School to Coláiste Therese was something of a shock to me. Coláiste Therese exposed me to the influence of students from all corners of Ireland including Northern Ireland. Not only did I find their accents strange to the ear and at times difficult to understand , but their varied backgrounds, rural and urban, were an awesome revelation to my young impressionable mind. This widening of experience, that liberal embrace of a multi-faceted world, is itself a quality I have always associated with the Presentation Brothers. Coláiste Therese was my first real taste of this breadth of vision.

Coláiste Therese was also experienced as a place of enormous energy. The teaching staff, composed for the most part of young Brothers studying at University College Cork, contributed in no small way to this liveliness. Their youthful supervision of energetic teenagers just a few years their junior certainly didn't evoke fear among their charges. Indeed, I feel it would be true to say that the Presentation tradition, and I'm convinced that there is such an entity, was, as far as I can attest, always fair and caring. As evidence of this I can point to my own situation in Coláiste Therese. On reflection, it seems a trifle odd to have been a boarder in a school at the other end of the avenue from my own home less than a half a mile away. Naturally, I was always more than willing to volunteer for the weekly trip to the post office on Bandon Road with the grimy and sweaty products of Sunday morning student letter-writing. I'm certain at this stage, looking back over time, that 'Presentation tolerance' frequently turned a blind eye to my regular forays 'over the wall' to home. Either that or they were enormously naive. I prefer to think that it was the former.

Following completion of my Leaving Certificate in Coláiste Therese the next step for me and for about twenty others was to Mount St Joseph in Blarney Street, Cork, there to spend five years firstly as a novice and then as a temporary professed Brother. I always believed that my real education took place during this period of my life. Certainly the three years of secondary schooling I spent at Coláiste Therese were, to say the least of it, somewhat rushed. Mount St Joseph, on the other hand, provided time and space for reflection and growth and for an emphasis on the spiritual dimensions of one's existence. There was, as you would expect, ample opportunity for silence and prayer, reading, study and contemplation. But there was also enormous stimulation and activity, from games and sports of all kinds to apple and potato picking, drama and elocution classes, glorious day trips to the seaside resorts of Garretstown and Owenahincha, sun-drenched weeks on Beare Island off the West Cork coast and, of course, yet more singing and music. The gramophone player in the novices' recreation room was a real Mecca for the many music worshippers but, strangely enough, what I recall most vividly in terms of music is not Val Doonican or Jim Reeves but the hauntingly evocative strains of the Gregorian Chant Mass for the Dead. The notes of the *In Paradisum* and the *Dies Irae* still come into my head at the most unexpected moments and my children are perplexed and confused when I break into Latin song around the house or in the car. Death, at that stage, seemed to have no dominion, and I, to my shame, actually enjoyed, with most of my fellow novices, the celebrations and feasting which accompanied funerals in the 'Mount'.

The camaraderie of these same fellow novices, some of whom became lifelong friends, was something I really treasured. Most of these, of course, had been classmates in Coláiste Therese, but we were also joined by novices from the West Indies and Canada and these added extra spice, zest and, dare I say, colour to proceedings. The atmosphere in Mount St Joseph, reflecting the tone and ethos of the Presentation Congregation itself, was, to my mind, relaxed, happy and supportive. There was, of course, a very definite discipline and sense of order pervading our daily lives but this was an understandable and necessary control, giving some semblance of decorum and 'smacht' to scores of young men bursting with youthful energy. This control, however, was counterbalanced by an increasing tendency on the part of many of us to question established norms and to think for ourselves. After all this was 'the Sixties'. John, Paul, Ringo and George were strutting their stuff on the world stage and two other Johns – John F. Kennedy and John XXIII – were breaking moulds and opening windows. While those charged with our care may not have exactly encouraged undue radicalism in us, to their great credit, they certainly didn't repress our honest questioning either. Indeed, as young temporary professed Brothers, we were actively encouraged to contribute to the Order's own discerning of the way forward in a modern world. The mould-shattering influence of the Vatican Council was everywhere to be felt in the Church and the documents of the Council, staple diet in our training at this period, left a marked and lasting impression on our minds.

During this period also we worked as 'unqualified' teachers in the Brothers' primary schools at Greenmount, Turner's Cross and the Mardyke. I stress the word 'unqualified': 'untrained' we most certainly were not. Indeed, the pedagogical training we received both in the schools themselves and in Mount St Joseph was, in my view, second to none. This programme of training, tightly monitored, professionally grounded, more activity-based than academic, made real teachers of us and concentrated our attention on what teaching is really all about: thorough preparation for classroom presentation, hard work on a daily basis and the focusing of the efforts of teacher and students on standards of excellence. I look back on this particular period of my life as fair 'seed-time' for a career of involvement in education. Certainly, I found secondary school teaching relatively easy after such a grounding at primary level. The trust which the Brothers had in us and, indeed, the sense of responsibility which they imparted to us, when one considers it, was breathtaking. Here I was at the age of seventeen with a class of more than fifty seven-year-olds for First Communion in Scoil Chríost Rí, Turner's Cross, Cork, leading the congregational singing in Christ the King Church at First Communion Mass on a May morning. The boys in the Leaving Certificate class in the adjoining Coláiste Chríost Rí were, for the most part, older than I was. My situation, I hasten to add, was by no means unique. There were, if my memory serves me right, five other young Brothers in a similar situation in Scoil Chríost Rí at the time and many others in the Brothers' other schools in Cork. We ourselves never believed that we were doing anything extraordinary. While we gave a lot in terms of time, energy and commitment, we gained far more in return. In modern day terms I feel that we had been 'empowered', surely the primary aim of all education.

Yet another Presentation experience at this stage in my life was in the Brothers, Junior Industrial School in West Grinstead, Sussex, England. Though I spent only one period of summer relief work there, it was a definite period of 'growing up', coming face-to-face with some of the harsher social realities after the relatively sheltered experiences of Cork. In West Grinstead I witnessed the positive influence of the Brothers on the lives of youngsters who had fallen foul of the law. This work, to my way of thinking, was most in keeping with the spirit of Edmund Rice's concern for the weakest and most marginalised in society. And yet, even here, there were some extremely happy moments which I can still vividly recall. I remember, for instance, being with a group of students from the school performing some Irish dancing at a very sedate and proper local Church of England summer garden fête. I'm not sure that our hosts knew exactly what to make of it all. After all, this was decades before *Riverdance* had glamourised and popularised Irish dancing on a world stage.

By the age of twenty the question of a lifelong religious vocation was one which was increasingly exercising my mind. Again, the generosity and understanding of the Brothers was exemplified in the opportunity and space they afforded me to spend a year teaching in Prince George, British Columbia, Canada, far away from comrades and colleagues, 'far from the madding crowd'. This gave me ample time to reflect on my own personal future. I left the Brothers amicably after much painful soul-searching at the end of my year in Canada, aged twenty-one. Four years later, after completing my studies in University College, Cork, I was back in the fold, as it were, teaching as a lay member of staff in Presentation College, Cork.

Here again the same Presentation motifs emerged – the liberal tradition in education; the encouragement to experiment and to innovate in the classroom, to try, succeed and even fail; the great social concern as exemplified in that most extraordinary of student organisations, SHARE; the emphasis on excellence and high standards in every aspect of the students' lives; and, most importantly, the real and genuine concern for each and every individual boy in the classroom. That 'vision', so important in energising all aspects of school life, was at times breathtaking in its audacity and boldness, making the school a pathfinder in many fields of educational innovation. In particular, at a personal level I fondly recall 'The Centenary Grand Tour' with eighty students to Rome, Florence, Antibes, Monaco, Switzerland and Paris. The sheer extent of such an adventure, celebrating a hundred years of Presentation College, Cork, was, to my mind, a mere reflection of that breadth of vision which vivified and informed so many other facets of school life.

The boys responded most positively to such a vision. I found in them a great pride in school, an integrity, honesty and forthrightness which at times was quite astonishing and occasionally caused raised eyebrows. Their sense of decency, fair play and justice is something I will always take with me. Presentation College was and, from what I gather from my own boys who now attend there, still is a happy school. This, in my view, is the ultimate tribute you can pay to any school. I like to think that the Presentation tradition, ethos, atmosphere, spirit – call it what you will – which comes down from Edmund but which is mediated through generations of Presentation Brothers and others in the wider Presentation family, is to be found in all Presentation schools, taking in each of them a form unique to that individual school.

As for myself, – well, I've moved on, as well I might, after twenty-two years of teaching. The transition hasn't been that difficult, merely into a related field of education with the Department of Education. But the Presentation spirit of tolerance, freedom, trust in people, excellence, caring and happiness which I witnessed with the Brothers along the road from Greenmount through Mount St Joseph, Turner's Cross, West Grinstead, Prince George and Presentation College, Mardyke, Cork, to the Department of Education still, I believe, informs many of my thoughts and actions. My ongoing interaction and contact with the Brothers through my Associate membership, through being secretary of the Presentation Association (Past Members of the Presentation Brothers) and through having two boys in Presentation College, Cork, ensures that I will not stray too far from their influence.

I believe in providence. I believe that we are destined to take a certain path through life and that though we ourselves may not always be certain of the exact and precise direction we are to take, certain coincidences and recurrences help us to discern the path destined for us. The Presentation Brothers have been one such coincidence and constant in my life. They have been there from the beginning. Somehow or other, at virtually every stage in my life, they have had a considerable influence on the shape my life has taken. And though I have not always been conscious of or, indeed, acknowledged this influence, it has always, thankfully, managed to reassert itself.

> There's a divinity that shapes our ends
> Rough-hew them how we will.
>
> (Hamlet v. ii.10)

THE PRESENTATION BROTHERS IN COBH

Declan Kennedy

Imagine attending school in a building with a panoramic view of one of finest natural harbours in the world. Imagine gazing out through the windows at the passing ships, at a magnificent Gothic cathedral and beautifully laid out gardens containing an orchard, greenhouses, flower beds and vegetable patches. This was the environment of learning in which the students of Presentation College, Cobh, were immersed.

Although Presentation College, Cobh, closed in 1976 and was incorporated into the new community school, Coláiste Muire, there still exists a very vibrant and active past pupils' union with a membership of 396 scattered throughout the globe. People outside of the Pres Cobh environs may wonder at this extraordinary fact but to the PPU members themselves it is a completely natural phenomenon. Pres Cobh had a very warm, intimate atmosphere in which there was a great love of learning and a deep respect for the Brothers and lay teachers who taught there. It is only natural that we should want to keep in touch with each other and ensure that the embers of friendship still glow warmly. Looking back at my formative years, it is clear to me that the Catholic ethos, the sense of fellowship and the warmth of good feeling were put in place and carefully nurtured by the Presentation Brothers themselves. The Brothers have served the people of Cobh since 1889 right down to the present day.

My earliest memories of the Brothers was not in the field of education but rather in a different type of field – in their garden! It was very common for the people of Cobh to visit the garden to 'buy' produce like vegetables, apples, rhubarb and so on. I remember as a very young lad being sent by my mother to collect produce from the Brothers' garden on Saturday mornings. At that time, about five or six Brothers would be happily occupied in various locations around the magnificent garden. The friendliness with which my companions and I were greeted will always remain with me. The marvellous generosity with which the Brothers filled baskets with items such as apples, rhubarb, lettuce, spring onions, for all who called will never be forgotten by the people of Cobh. A token few pennies is all they would accept as payment. The Christian charity of Edmund Rice was clearly visible to the people of Cobh.

I spent ten wonderful years being educated by the Presentation Brothers: five in St Joseph's National School and five in Pres Cobh. In all those years the one thing that impressed me most was their self-sacrifice. They gave so willingly of their time in the area of extra tuition, sports, school tours, etc. that it was a privilege to be taught by them. I feel that this was the key to the warm atmosphere that pervaded the school. The fact that we interacted with the Brothers outside the strict discipline of the classroom helped us to appreciate the kindness and humanity of these men. In addition, it was very clear to us that they always had our welfare at heart and worked hard to help us pursue our chosen careers. This ensured that the sense of unity of purpose between teacher and student – the essence of the educational process – was placed on a very firm footing.

There were no school secretaries or caretakers in those days! I often recall stray footballs crashing through panes of glass during the morning break. The glass would be replaced without any fuss by one of the Brothers after school hours. At break time the Brothers would stroll around the grounds chatting with us. Career Guidance teachers did not exist at the time. I remember Brother Vincent (my Latin teacher) asking me what I intended to do when I left school. I told him that I hoped to become a teacher of my favourite subject – Latin. To my surprise he advised me against studying Latin at university and told me my job prospects would be far better if I opted to study Chemistry and Physics instead. His advice was among the best I ever got and I have received enormous pleasure from teaching these subjects over the past twenty years.

On reflecting on my education, I look back with warm affection at the great men of the Presentation Order with whom I was privileged to have come in contact: Brothers Celsus, Thaddeus, Paul, Chrysostom, Urban, Polycarp, Declan, Aidan and Raphael, all of whom I knew in primary school. On moving into secondary school I was fortunate to have had gifted teachers like Brother Vincent, who instilled in me a great love of Latin, and Brother Callistus whose mathematical brilliance ensured that I was well-prepared for my chosen career in science. Brother Clement was a very kind Principal and Brother Theodore ensured that we all learned the meaning of the word discipline!

One of the greatest events in my life was that, on returning to Coláiste Muire as a student teacher, I was fortunate enough to work under Brother Bede as Principal. His kindness, helpfulness, hard work and total dedication were an inspiration to me. It was an honour and a privilege to have worked with him and I shall be eternally grateful to him for all that he has taught me. In more recent years, it was also wonderful to work with Brothers Martin and Bertrand. Moreover, during the past year, Brother Walter has been welcomed with joy to our staff at Coláiste Muire, Cobh.

It would be remiss of me not to mention the marvellous lay teachers of Pres Cobh with whom the Presentation Brothers forged such a great partnership. Of these lay teachers two giants of men stand out – Con Hamilton and Maurice O'Brien. The fact that over three hundred past pupils gathered to pay tribute to them in 1986 is sufficient testimony to the high regard in which they were held.

Over the past number of years there have been many events organised by the PPU which have clearly demonstrated the high esteem in which the Presentation Brothers are held by their past pupils and by the people of Cobh. In 1989 a beautiful limestone plaque was unveiled on the site where Presentation College was founded on 12 August 1889. A centenary booklet charting the history of Pres Cobh was also produced by the PPU. A special centenary Mass and function were held at which the guest speaker, Dr Chris Walsh, who had travelled from California, gave a truly brilliant address in praise of Presentation College. A photographic tribute tracing the contribution of the Brothers in Cobh was mounted in Coláiste Muire in 1994 to mark the 150th anniversary of the death of Edmund Rice. A special award was also instituted in the school in his honour. A number of activities are being organised at local level by the PPU to celebrate the beatification of Edmund Rice, including a special Mass and celebratory function, sponsorship of public speaking awards in Coláiste Muire, setting up an Awards Ceremony in St Joseph's National School, the unveiling of a commemorative plaque and the naming of a new housing estate in honour of Edmund Rice.

In all of the activities in which the members of the PPU are involved there is one word that always comes to mind – gratitude. Gratitude for the education we have received, gratitude for the values nurtured within us during our formative years, gratitude for the selfless dedication of the men of the Presentation Order whose example was an inspiration that has endured down the years and who gave so much to ensure that Pres Cobh is remembered with such warm affection.

Looking at the work initiated in Cobh in the name of Edmund Rice, and carried on for more than a century by his followers, the Presentation Brothers, there is a quotation from the poet Horace that sums it up well: *nexegi monumentum perennius aere* – I have built a monument more lasting than bronze.

THE DINGBAT'S SONG
Greg Delanty

Memory, that moody master composer,
    washes up the bleeding pages & gutters
    and deftly makes a dummy of me as I set
        and reset Eagle Printing Company
    and the characters who lined its floors,
struggling with the type of undone galleys
thrown without a word into the hellbox.

*

Now I'm stuck like the bastard type,
    cast from that place & those letters
    and must set myself in this new world,
        quitting the search for those lost
    characters to assure me I can start
the next awkward paragraph without them
and not make myself a perpetual dingbat.

AS THE CIRCLE TURNS....

Kieran Groeger

Education is what is left when all that you have been taught in school is forgotten. It is not, contrary to what many people think, that extra bit of polish, the fine word, the good manners. Sophistication in dress or speech amounts to little more than a veneer, while education is more of a residue, a hard core value which remains when all else is stripped away.

I am, or rather was, a Pres boy who has in the recent past become a lay principal of a Christian Brothers' (CBS) school. This has posed serious problems of identity for me, not to mention a conflict of loyalties. It is not quite on the same level as the predicament Denis Law found himself in when he was playing for Manchester City, but it's not far from it. Pres and Christians have shared a mutual rivalry that has been nurtured within each school for generations.

I have now spent some years with the Presentation Brothers, some years with the De La Salle Brothers and am currently with the Christian Brothers. It can be confusing. Why, for example, do Pres Brothers use Christian names while Christian Brothers use surnames? One gets used to Brother Martin, Brother Matthew and Brother Carthage and then one meets Brother Collins, Brother Vaughan and Brother O'Mahony. Not to mention the ever slumbering Frère Jacques about whom we sang in several languages! And, in the background, there is, of course, Brother Rice, who is sometimes Brother Ignatius. But why the difference? Was it a conscious decision to keep a surname or to adopt a religious name?

Looking at the life of a religious order as a great circle, it would appear that it is coming fuel circle and a future generation of followers of Edmund Rice may well be like the first – a group of dedicated laymen with a passion and zeal to espouse his work. Perhaps we are that generation, perhaps it is yet to come. God alone knows at what point on the circle we are situated. As a lay principal, I feel a strong need to ensure that the school will continue in the tradition of Edmund Rice and, in so doing, I look back at my own experience of being educated by his followers.

This, for me, was the bulk of my primary education when I became a skull-capped, purple-blazered, short-panted and large school-bagged Pres boy, with an American style crew cut, a small blonde fringe and big blue eyes. Cork people knew me well – there were thousands of me tramping along the Western Road in the late 1950s and early 1960s, all with big gaps where our teeth used to be before the fatal visit to the dentist at the City Hall. 'I got nine out, how about you'? We compared and boasted about our edentate state and still bought slabs of toffee from Campbell's shop and broke them on our knee and it didn't really hurt at all.

A conviction of belonging to a great school, with a great tradition, with definite values was part of being a Pres Boy. This conviction was drilled into us in the school yard before matches when cheerleaders trained the supporters and members of the team were paraded like heroes.

> Tango! Tango Wallah Wallah Miskey.
> Yerawaddy! Yerawaddy! Yup Yup Yup!
> Horum Harum Kwee Kwee Kee
> Jasper Jasper P. B. C. !!!

We chanted now in unison, then in harmony. We prepared paper hats, we made buntings, we made flags. We learned our songs, our chants, our choruses: 'We love our name, our glorious name, For Pres we'll do or die'. And we meant it! Double-decker bus-loads of stark raving lunatic supporters all in black, white and purple. Musgrave Park here we come!

'Two, four, six, eight – who do we appreciate?' we roared with vigour and with passion. It was unthinkable to return from a match and not be hoarse!

By the time the match started, we were already higher than kites, roaring on the team, drowning out the opposition. Some carried enormous teddy bears, others top hats. Many parents came to support the school: it was a social occasion and almost a formal one. If I have one abiding memory of being a Pres Boy, it is of the need for respect for others. At that rugby match, there was an expectation of total silence when the opposition took a penalty kick. It wasn't done to disrupt play by shouting. And so the silence, the breath holding. Then the gasp as the ball went over the bar, or the sigh of relief when it missed. We lived the game, we felt the game. We loved our name, our glorious name – 'For Pres we'll do or die' was our anthem. And we believed it!

The expectation of dignity extended to behaviour in and out of school. I remember an incident, when, as a child, I hurled less than ecumenical words at schoolboys attending a non-Catholic school nearby and a tearful, remorseful smart alec was obliged to apologise to the offended parties.

And yes – there were slaps , and yes – they were deserved, and yes – we accepted them without question. We felt somehow manly at our ability to take punishment without tears and no – it was not excessive for the time. Oh yes ! we talked about it, we knew about other schools where punishment was terrible but not ours; and no – our parents did not complain, and no – we did not consider the slaps unfair. We deserved them. It was the culture of the time, we knew no different way; perhaps our teachers knew no different either. It seemed almost natural – boys will be boys, boys will be boisterous, boys will get into trouble, boys will be punished, life goes on! Today, for teachers as well as students, there are endless forms, warnings, notes home, exclusions, intricate and sophisticated disciplinary systems. Is it any better? Many a teacher and perhaps many a student would prefer a once-off slap hoping, like Macbeth, 'that but this blow Might be the be all and the end all – here.'

And there are memories: of verse speaking competitions at Feis Maitiú when I had the honour of being Captain of the Presentation College Verse Speaking team and we won and I won the only medal I ever got in my entire school life; and rugby, and musicals – especially a wonderful Gilbert and Sullivan tradition and Christopher Robin kneeling at his bedside, saying his prayers; and rugby and variety shows; and rugby and drill sessions in white flannels; and rugby and picking stones to clear the new pitch in Bishopstown; and more memories of rugby, and more rugby and more rugby and even when I went to the Bon Secour

Hospital to have my tonsils out, a kindly doctor asked me to blow up a rugby ball in the theatre because he 'knew Pres boys loved rugby', and 'Yes, Doctor I'll try zzzzzz'.

Did I mention rugby? I should – it was important, although I never got to wear the jersey myself. The nearest I ever got to being part of the rugby team was when I was once, and once only, asked to be a linesman at a match in Clanwilliam. I was told that one hand in the air and the other outstretched at right angles indicated the side to which the line-out was awarded. My coordination and judgement were suspect and probably slightly inaccurate as, after a few minutes, the referee kindly asked me to get something from the dressing-room. He said it might have fallen on the floor. I did as he told me and searched, and searched, but there wasn't any spare pea for his whistle and the match was nearly over before I gave up. He didn't seem to mind!

It may appear strange that one's abiding memories of primary school are largely out of class experiences. There are occasional glimpses, into the past, of mental arithmetic, which I loved, of drill sessions in those white flannel long pants, of reading Biggles, the Famous Five, the Secret Seven, of poems learned by heart, of the Primary Cert examination, but the memories are vague, the details skimpy. I remember a gaberdine coat but it never rained – or did it? I hardly remember the names of teachers, the place in class where I sat, some friends yes, enemies – did I have any? I don't know. What endures is the conviction, the passion, the sense of pride associated with being a Pres boy and the standards which were held out for us to carry into adult life.

And so my education as a Pres boy is largely composed of all those things which I was taught but have forgotten, and ideas I picked up through being there but which were not formally taught. And where was the shadow of Edmund Rice in all this? I like to think that the education I received in Pres would have met with his approval. I think he would have been aware of the hidden curriculum and praised the values we brought with us. After all, education is what remains when all you have learned in the classroom is forgotten.

THE STRANGER
Greg Delanty

The sun drops quietly into McSorleys, hesitates
at the doorway as if perusing the joint, decides
it's okay and slips up next to you at the bar
like a stranger who thankfully keeps to himself —
He leaves you alone to draft some old poem
about the ghosts of Micks who strayed in,
thirsty & alone, on another day such as this
of another century and who still drift here
like the full stops of dust spotlit by the sun
haloing the heads of the Yankee-capped drinkers
swigging gold that could be the alchemist's elixir —
Something lifts and suddenly you haven't a care
and you're sure if you look at your page that all
the periods have ascended here into the air

PRESENTATION COLLEGE, CORK, REMEMBERED

Fergal Keane

I cannot say that I remember my first day very clearly but I certainly remember the last. We were days away from the first exams of the Leaving Certificate and the reality of a life in the adult world beyond the gates was looming. The boisterousness and high spirits of the previous weeks, the demob happy atmosphere that always accompanies the end of a school year had given way to a more sober feeling. Now we knew that the structures within which we had lived for years were about to evaporate. The days measured out in the ringing of a school bell were disappearing.

There were quite a few who at the time rejoiced loudly at escaping from school. It was the kind of thing one was expected to do – make exaggerated gestures and loud denunciations of the place we were leaving behind. And yet beneath our callow yelps and shouts, beneath the pranks and jokes, many of us felt the first faint tinges of regret as we walked out the gates and turned left towards the noise of the city. It was a sentiment born not simply out of fear for what the future held, but, in my case at least, also out of an abiding fondness for Pres. My schooldays, however, were by no means trouble-free.

In my first year I had the distinction of being suspended twice – once more and I would have been expelled. I have vivid memories of a dark winter's evening clearing rubbish on the Mardyke in the company of Michael Kiernan, both of us having been thrown out of a science class for talking. Our headmaster, Brother Jerome, did not believe in beating his pupils – he was much more subtle and intelligent in his handling of miscreants like myself and Mick Kiernan. Several hours painstakingly clearing the Mardyke of crisp packets and cigarette butts was an infinitely more daunting prospect than any clip around the ear.

In those early days of secondary school I was a far from perfect pupil. I talked too much in class, I went on the 'hop', I never seemed to have my homework done on time. There were any number of frantic 'cogging' sessions in the yard as the bell time approached. Yet, to his credit, Brother Jerome saw all of this for what it was: the struggle of a confused teenager trying to find out who he was. He took a personal interest in my progress, encouraging me to take part in school activities, warning me off when I strayed from what he saw as the wise path. I can truthfully say that I would not be where I am today without Brother Jerome. It is a debt I am only too happy to acknowledge publicly .

The Pres of those years lives in my memory as an enlightened school where education of the whole person was paramount. Yes, academic results were given a high priority, but not obsessively so. We were encouraged to take part in sports, drama and debating. The latter was a particular favourite of mine and made a major contribution to giving me the confidence so necessary in my present occupation. In English and History, the teaching of men like Pat Coffey and Declan Healy brought the subjects alive for me and deepened my determination to find a career that allowed me to make daily use of both. In my less brilliant – to put it mildly – subjects like Maths and Commerce, I can only thank the forbearance of Donal O'Brien and Mick Hennessy. They knew that I would never enjoy or be any good at their subjects, but they did their best for me. They will be happy to know that my maths and accounting skills have improved dramatically: having to negotiate contracts and expenses with the BBC revealed hidden numerical skills!

What I also cherish is what I will call the 'civilised' atmosphere. Pres was never a place of fear and terror. One did not approach the headmaster's office in dread of physical violence. Yes, there was discipline but, as I mentioned earlier, it was, by and large, applied with subtlety. That Brother Jerome had a will of iron nobody could doubt, but he inspired respect, not fear. The official disapproval of physical violence helped to create and nurture an atmosphere of mutual respect. Having witnessed so much hurt and destruction as a war correspondent, I am more convinced than ever that in schools, as indeed everywhere else, we must avoid violence.

After an uncertain start I came to thoroughly enjoy school. I made friends at Pres who still remain my best friends. I formed a rock-and-roll band with my classmates and I met my first real girlfriend. (I saw her for the first time at one of Brother Jerome's famous Pres discos! She too remains a good friend.) I got my first taste of democracy when I stood for election as a prefect and learned some considerable negotiating skills during our perfects' meetings with Brother Jerome. I had my first taste of radio and television working in the groundbreaking 'Pres' Studios. I joined SHARE and became heavily involved its programmes to help the elderly. SHARE in particular helped to raise my awareness of the inequalities in our society, an awareness that has had a lasting impact on my work as a journalist.

The work done by SHARE and the continual reminders from Brother Jerome about our social responsibilities were for me the best answer to those who criticised Pres as elitist or snobbish. In every civics or religious instruction class we were reminded that we had a responsibility to side with those who were powerless. Perhaps most importantly, we were encouraged to think and to question. Anybody who thinks the Jesuits have a monopoly on the skills of argument and debate has clearly never experienced the Presentation Brothers in full flight.

Although much of what I have written here concerns very serious matters, my abiding memories of Pres are of laughter with good friends and the discovery of ideas and principles. And although I am by nature inclined to avoid what might be termed the establishment, I am always proud to say that I was, and indeed am, a Pres boy.

THE CONTRIBUTORS

Coffey, Pat: born in Cork. Educated at Greenmount Primary School, Coláiste Therese and UCC. Taught in Ireland and Canada at primary and secondary level. He is at present a Post-Primary Inspector with the Department of Education and is based in Cork. Pat is married to Josephine, who is also a post-primary teacher, and they have three children.

Conroy, Joseph A.: born in Cork in 1863. Entered Greenmount Orphanage on the death of his father in 1871, remaining until 1878. On leaving at the age of fifteen, he became a monitor (trainee teacher), first in the South Monastery, Douglas Street, Cork, and later in the Lancasterian School, Cork. A young man of exemplary industry and self-discipline, he intended to become a Presentation Brother but lack of success in the classroom convinced him that his vocation lay elsewhere. He emigrated to Philadelphia where he married and had a family. He always remained attached to the Presentation Brothers and gave some of them a great welcome when they later visited his adopted city. He wrote several pamphlets of a broad educational nature.

Cremin, Jim: born in Cork. Educated at Greenmount Primary School, Coláiste Chríost Rí and University College, Cork. Represented his school and UCC in hurling. Won many hurling honours and trophies including Harty, Munster and All-Ireland minor medals with Cork; Senior and Fitzgibbon medals with UCC and numerous medals with his club, Nemo Rangers. After a period working as an industrial chemist, he joined the staff of Coláiste Chríost Rí as a science teacher. In addition

to teaching, he coaches college and club GAA teams, is interested in the Irish language and in under-achieving students. He is also the author of a book for students on health care and personal development.

Delanty, Greg: born in Cork. Educated at Scoil Chríost Rí and Coláiste Chríost Rí, Cork, and UCC. In addition to having individual poems published in numerous journals and editing three anthologies of poetry, he has published the following poetry collections: *Cast in the Fire* (1986), *Southward* (1992), *American Wake* (1996). A further collection, *The Hellbox,* is in progress. He has also been the recipient of several honours and awards including the Allan Dowling Poetry Fellowship and the

Wolfer O'Neill Foundation Literary Award 1996. Greg is Poet-in-Residence and lecturer at St Michael's College, Winooski, Canada.

(Photo: Bohadan Zinczenko)

Donovan, Daniel C.: born in Ballincollig, Co. Cork, in 1926. Educated at Presentation College, Cork, 1932-44 and at UCC where he obtained the degrees of BA, MA and HDipEd. He joined staff of his old school in 1947. He is co-founder of the Presentation Theatre Guild and has also worked as actor, producer and director with several theatre groups in Cork, including Comhantas Chorcaí, Theatre of the South, Everyman Theatre and Everyman Palace Theatre. Retired from teaching as Vice-Principal of Presentation College, Cork.

Feheney, John Matthew: born in Co. Limerick in 1932. Entered Presentation Brothers in 1948. Educated at Presentation Brothers, Cork, UCC, UWI, University of London. He is the Director of the Christian Formation Resource Centre, Cork. His publications include *Pastoral Care*, 3 vols (1994), *Education and the Family* (1995), *Edmund Rice 150th Anniversary Yearbook* (1995), *O'Shaughnessys of Munster* (1996) and many articles in journals.

Fraher, John: born in Cork. Educated at Presentation College, and UCC, where he qualified in medicine and science, and the University of Edinburgh (PhD & DSc). Lecturer in anatomy at Edinburgh (1968-75) and at the University of London (1975-78). Professor of Anatomy at UCC (1978). Currently visiting professor and Research Fellow at the Karolinska Institute, Stockholm, and the University of Uppsala. He is an anatomist and neuroscientist. His main research interest is the  central nervous system and its basic structural biology as related to multiple sclerosis and the treatment of stroke.

Galvin, Patrick: born in Cork in 1927. Educated at South Monastery school, Cork. He has been writing poetry and drama since his early years and has been a frequent broadcaster of his own work on RTE and BBC. He has been Resident Dramatist at Lyric Theatre, Belfast (1974-78), and a writer-in-residence in England. His plays have been widely performed and broadcast in Ireland, England, Canada, USA and France. In addition to his poetry collections, stage and radio plays, he has also record-  ed seven collections of Irish street ballads. He has published two volumes of autobiography, *Song for a Poor Boy* (1991) and *Song for a Raggy Boy* (1992). His forthcoming *New and Selected Poems* will be published later this year by Cork University Press.

Groeger, Kieran: born in Cork. Educated at Presentation College, Coláiste Iosagáin and UCC. He is Principal of CBS Secondary School, Youghal, and an active member of Cork Principals and Vice-Principals Association. He is currently reading for a PhD in education with CFRC/University of Hull. He is married to Bríd with three children.

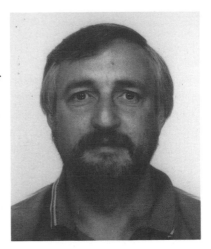

Hurwitz, Cecil: born in Cork. Educated at Presentation College and UCC (BA, HDipEd). Taught at CBS Fermoy and CBS Midleton. Founded PEACE Movement (Prayer, Enterprise and Christian Effort) in 1974 and works for peace and reconciliation in Ireland. He is the author of four books: *History: Leaving Cert Modern Course: Questions and Answers; From Synagogue to Church: An Autobiography; Mind Your Ps and Qs: A Comprehensive List of Proverbs and Quotations; Bible Quiz: The Old Testament.*

Keane, Fergal: born in Cork. Educated at Presentation College. Showed an early interest in journalism and started his career as a reporter on *The Limerick Leader.* From there he moved to the *Irish Press*, then to RTE and later to the BBC. He is now BBC Asia Correspondent based in Hong Kong. Prior to that he was BBC Southern Africa correspondent and Ireland correspondent. He has been named Journalist of the Year by the Royal Television Society, Reporter of the Year in the Sony Radio  Awards, Amnesty International Human Rights Reporter of the Year and he recently won the George Orwell Prize for Non-Fiction for his book on Rwanda, *Season of Blood.* He is married to Anne Flaherty and they have one son, Daniel.

Kelleher, Michael J.: born in Cork. Educated at Presentation College, UCC, where he qualified in medicine, and at London University. He is a consultant psychiatrist at Maudsley and Bethlem Royal Hospitals; lecturer in Psychiatry at University College, Cork; Clinical Director of Psychiatric Services in North Lee catchment area, Southern Health Board. He has published numerous scientific articles and several books, his most recent being, *Suicide and the Irish* (1996). Michael is a member of the  editorial board of the journals *Irish Journal of Psychiatry, Archives of Suicide Research* and *Crisis.*

Kennedy, Declan: born in Cobh. Educated at Presentation Brothers Primary School, Presentation College, Cobh, and UCC, where he studied chemistry. He teaches at Coláiste Muire, Cobh, and is the author of several science school texts, including *Science Today* (1985), *Science for the Future* (1990), and *The World of Science* (1995). He is an active member of Irish Science Teachers Association and secretary of Presentation College, Cobh, PPU.

Lucky, Anthony: born in Trinidad and educated at Presentation College, San Fernando, University of the West Indies and Lincoln's Inn, London. Called to the Bar (Trinidad) and practised as a barrister; appointed to the secretariat of the Law Reform Commission; appointed magistrate, then judge of Circuit Court before his present appointment as judge of the Supreme Court of Trinidad and Tobago. Anthony is married to Cyntra with two daughters.

Mac Mathúna, Liam: born in Broadford, Co. Limerick in 1911. Educated at Presentation Brothers, Cork, De La Salle Teacher's College, Waterford, and UCC. He has had a lifelong interest in the Irish language (holder of Sár-Theastas). Principal of St Brendan's NS, Birr, and St Brendan's NS, Limerick, up to retirement. He was associated with St Finbarr's Hurling Club, Cork, during his early years in Cork.

Maher, Sean.: born in 1932 of traveller parents. Entered St Joseph's Industrial School, Cork, in 1944, where, after learning to read and write, he discovered his great thirst for knowledge. His longing for education came to an end, however, when his father insisted that he leave school at sixteen to go 'on the road'. His mother tried in various ways to get him into a trade but his father opposed it, announcing to his mother, 'Your darling scholar son will have to get used to mooching (begging) now; his holiday is over; and if he doesn't, I'll break his back.' His autobiographical *The Road to God Knows Where* was published by The Talbot Press in 1972.

McGahern, John: born in 1934 in County Leitrim where he still lives and works a small farm. Educated at Presentation College, Carrick-on-Shannon and St Patrick's College, Drumcondra. He was a primary teacher until 1966 when his second novel, *The Dark*, was banned and he was dismissed by the clerical authorities. His novels include *The Barracks* (1963); *The Dark* (1965); *The Leavetaking* (1975); *The Pornographer* (1980) and *Amongst Women* (1990). He has also published several short story collections  as well as works for radio and television and has won numerous literary awards. His work has appeared in many anthologies and his novels and short stories have been translated into many languages.

Nolan, Liam: born in Cobh in 1932. Educated at Presentation Brothers National School and Presentation College, Cobh. He joined the BBC in 1953 and worked as BBC sports reporter and later as presenter of *Sports Report* and *Today* programmes. He also worked with ITV before returning to RTE to present *The Liam Nolan Hour*. He won many awards in radio and TV, including the Jacobs Award and International Truth Award (US). Liam is now working on his fourteenth book. He is married to Oonagh and they have four children.

O'Faolain, Sean: born in Cork in 1900, son of an RIC constable. Educated at Lancasterian school, Presentation College, UCC and Harvard University. In 1932 he became a founding member of the Irish Academy of Letters, along with Shaw, Yeats and other literary figures of the time. During the early 1940s he was editor of the distinguished literary journal, *The Bell*. His publications include four novels, numerous short stories and five biographies, as well as works of travel and literary criticism. He died in 1991 and is regarded as one of Ireland's foremost men of letters.

Steele, Frank: born in Cork. Educated at North Monastery, Marino Institute of Education, UCC (BA, MA, HDipEd) and Keble College, Oxford (DPhil). He is Principal of St Aidan's Community College, Cork, and a lecturer and tutor for the MEd course in University of Hull/CFRC. He is author of *Towards a Spirituality for Layfolk* (1995). Frank is married to Mary and they have two children.

Titley, Alan: born in Cork, in 1947. Educated at Scoil Chríost Rí and Coláiste Chríost Rí, Cork, St Patrick's College, Drumcondra, and UCD. He taught and travelled in Africa in 1967-69 and taught deaf children for a time before joining the staff of St Patrick's College, Drumcondra, where he is Head of the Irish Department. He is the author of many books in Irish and English as well as a writer and presenter of radio and TV programmes in both languages. He is the recipient of Oireachtas prizes for several

forms of writing: the Pater Prize, Butler Prize and the numerous Arts Council Bursaries. He is the Irish language editor of *Books Ireland* and presenter of an RTE Radio book programme in Irish. Alan is married to Mary Fitzgerald and they have five children.

Van Esbeck, Edmund: born in Cork and educated at Presentation College, Mardyke. He is rugby correspondent for *The Irish Times* and author of several books including: *One Hundred Years of Irish Rugby* (1974); *The Irish Rugby Scrapbook* (1976); *The Story of Irish Rugby* (1986) and *Willie John* (McBride) (1976). He has also written centenary histories of Cork Constitution RFC, Monkstown RFC, Old Wesley RFC, and the Golden Jubilee History of Old Belvedere.

Wall, William: born at Whitegate in Co. Cork and educated at CBS Midleton and UCC, he now teaches English at Presentation College, Cork. He won the Patrick Kavanagh Award in 1995, the Listowel Writers Award for Poetry and the American-Ireland Foundation Writer's Week Poetry Prize in 1996. His first collection of poems, *Mathematics,* and a children's novel, *The Powder Monkey,* are due to be published later this year. He is married to Liz, who also teaches in Presentation College, Cork. They have two children.